Abide in Love the Sacred Presence of God
Meditative Prayer for Spiritual Care

Living in the Spirit of God

Frances Stroh RN, MA, FCN

Photographic Imagery by Joseph R. Reed & F. Stroh

TOLCARE
Touch of Life Care

Caring, Counseling, Education, Information
Books
Established 1991

http://www.franstroh.com/

http://www.tolcare.com/

Copyright © 2015 Frances Stroh, RN, MA, FCN

All rights reserved.

ISBN: 1514178397
ISBN-13: 978-1514178393

Dedication and Appreciation

Acknowledgments: Photography by Joseph R. Reed

Sincere Appreciation and Thank you to my grandson Joseph R. Reed for his expert technical support, assistance and outstanding photography.

Dedication and Thank you to God, My Angels, my Family, All my Children, Grandchildren, Friends and all who wish to Image and Experience Gods Holy Light in Meditative Prayer

Special Thank You and Appreciation to Rachel Little RN, MSN, FCN, and Anna-Maria Schaefer, FNP, BSN, for their assistance as co-presenters of Meditative Prayer for Spiritual Care at the Faith Community Nursing Westberg Symposium 2015

About the Book / Introduction

Abide in Love the Sacred Presence of God, Meditative Prayer for Spiritual Care

"Beloved, let us love one another, for love is from God; and everyone who loves is born of God and knows God. The one who does not love does not know God, for God is love." (1 John 4:7-8) (1) Abide in Love and Live in the Spirit of God's Peace. This is a sacred mission. God is asking each of us right now and eternally to Love each other regardless of differences. Let God's Holy Light Shine into the darkness and awaken to Sacred Peace.

A way to Spiritual Blessedness is written within our mind by God and becomes available as we Pray and Meditate. "Religious and spiritual practices such as meditation, prayer, and touch are reported to lengthen life, improve the quality of life, and improve health outcomes by enhancing psychological, physical and spiritual well-being. This is based on research reports in nursing literature and publications of other health professionals, as well as the professional literature focused on health ministry, chaplaincy, theology, spirituality, spiritual care, and pastoral care."(5)

We learn to practice methods of providing Spiritual Care through the use of Meditative Prayer that, in addition to the health and healing benefits, leads to Spiritual Growth and Inner Peace. The purpose of Meditative Prayer is to prepare our mind to enter into a state of meditation and contemplation in which we experience the Holy Presence of God in the Present Moment. It is Entering the Silence of the Mind. It is being at one with God. Meditation always begins with prayer to protect, help, guide and extend the blessings and the Peace of God. Seeds of Holy Inspiration, and trust in Gods power, are planted within our mind and soul. Meditative Prayer is a means in which we experience peace leading to recognition that all are God's children and United in Love.

Relaxation, imagery, visualization and centering during meditative prayer lead to a quiet clear mind that is receptive to Divine Intervention. There are multiple paths and ways to find the Peace of God's Holy Presence. During Meditative Prayer there is increasing awareness that we are a living temple of God's Love, Peace and Truth. All pathways of Love direct us to One Divine Presence and Sacred Peace. As we begin Meditative Prayer, receive God's Blessings of Spiritual Care for Mind, Heart and Soul. The Light of God, is with us as we pray and leads to being loving, forgiving, patient, kind, compassionate, tolerant, and joyful. "Blessed is the man who's ... ...delight is in the law of the Lord, and on his law he meditates day and night. He is like a tree planted by streams of water that yields its fruit in its season, and its leaf does not wither. In all that he does, he prospers." (Psalm 1:1-5) (1)

Nurses, health care providers, care givers and each person requires Spiritual Care that is given and received with unconditional Love for all people regardless of religion, belief or anything that separates us from each other and the Love of God. Our purpose is to promote peace and unity. The methods presented in this book are intended for all people. The information contains specific religious and spiritual data related to Christianity and various beliefs. God is to be understood as that which represents the Divine to you. We each have different beliefs but empathy and understanding for all is of vital importance for Living in the Spirit of God's Peace.

The Golden Rule is to Love and treat others the way we want to be treated. It is an ethical code that has created most of humanity's morality. Its earliest appearance begins in ancient wisdom manuscripts and teachings in Chinese, Egyptian and Greek cultures and it is found in virtually all the world's religious beliefs. In Christian and Jewish beliefs, the Golden Rule is stated to be the heart of all religious education. Jesus was asked what we must do to attain eternal life, the answer is "You shall love the Lord your God with all your heart and with all your soul and with all your strength and with all your mind, and your neighbor as yourself" (Luke 10:27) (1)

"If I speak with the tongues of men and of angels, but have not love, I am become sounding brass, or a clanging cymbal. And if I have the gift of prophecy, and know all mysteries and all knowledge; and if I have all faith, so as to remove mountains, but have not love, I am nothing. And if I bestow all my goods to feed the poor, and if I give my body to be burned, but have not love, it profited me nothing." (1 Corinthians 13) (1)

"Be still, and know that I am God. I will be exalted among the nations, I will be exalted in the earth!" (Psalm 46:10) (1)

Contents

Living in the Holy Spirit of God's Love	xiii
Living in the Spirit of God	xvii
In the Beginning There is Love	xvii
Components of Life and Conscious Existence	xviii
Spiritual Healing of the Whole Self	xxi
Holistic Health Care	xxiii
Managing Stress through Faith	xxiii
The Relaxation Process	xxv
Mental Imagery Hypnotic Effect	xxvi
Contemplation	xxviii
Meditation Defined	xxix
Preparing for Meditative Prayer	xxx
Centering Prayer	xxx
Divine Reading	xxxi
Christian Meditation	xxxi
Meditative Prayer Imagery	xxxii
Creating a Prescription for Spiritual Healing	xxxii
Prescription for Relaxation	xxxiii
Meditative Prayer Imagery Prescriptions	xxxiv
Prepare to Relax	xxxv
Focus Only on the Good	xxxv
Begin with Prayer	xxxvi
Rest in the Presence of God	xxxvi
1. Ascending in the Holy Spirit	1
Reception of Spiritual Gifts for Healing the Soul	3
Ascending in the Spirit of God	4
2. Entrance to God's Holy Place of Peace	7
Passage to Stillness for Healing the Mind	9
3. The Spirit of Renewed Life	11
Renewal of the Spiritual Self	12
4. Healing of the Heart	15
Unconditional Love for Healing of the Heart	17

5. Supportive Spiritual Care	19
The Reception of Spiritual Care	21
6. Healing Spirit	23
Meditative Prayer for Spiritual Healing	25
7. Realization of Wholeness	27
Spiritual Wholeness	29
8. The Compassionate Way	33
Feeling of Compassion	34
9. The Nature of a Loving God	37
Emotional Healing of the Heart	39
10. Our Angel Guardians	41
Touched by Angelic Light	43
11. Sacred Awareness	45
Develop a Sense of Sacred Awareness	47
12. Bridge of Heavenly Light	49
Finding God's Heavenly Light	51
13. Spiritual Care of the Soul	53
Spiritual Care of the Soul for Holy Presence	55
14. Living in the Spirit of God's Forgiveness	57
Forgiveness for Living in the Spirit of God	58
15. Spiritual Care of the Heart	61
Care of the Heart and Soul	63
16. Knowledge of Self	65
Knowledge of your Spiritual Self	66
17. Consciousness of the Spirit	69
A Spiritual Dimension of Consciousness	72
18. Raise up Your Soul	75
Homecoming of the Soul	77

19. The Spiritual Self	79
Awareness of your Spiritual Self	80
20. Sacred Gateway to Justification	85
Sacred Justification	89
21. Inner Reflection of God's Holy Presence	91
Inner Reflection within the Flow of Living	92
22. Transforming Care of the Soul	95
Transformational Healing	96
23. Sanctified Perception of Reality	99
Sanctified Perception	100
24. Flow of Spirit for Life	103
Flow of Life Giving Spirit	105
25. Spiritual Healing	107
Healing in the Holy Spirit of God	108
26. Unity in the Holy Spirit	111
Unity in the Spirit of God	113
27. The Presence of Guardian Angels	115
Awareness of the Presence of Angels	116
28. Spiritual Union	119
Healing through Spiritual Union	121
29. A Compassionate Spirit	123
Compassion in the Spirit of God	124
30. Serenity of the Soul	127
Sacred Serenity	129
31. Living in the Moment with God	131
In the Moment with God	133
32. Eternally in Remembrance	135
Forever in Memory	136
A Gift of Remembrance	137

33. Creative Light of God	139
Renewal of Spirit in the Light of God	140
34. The Flow and Breath of Life	143
Breath of Life for Healing	145
35. Home Living in the Spirit of God	147
Finding Our Heavenly Home	149
36. Living in the Spirit of God's Peace	153
Meditative Prayer for Peace	156
Sacred Reading	156
Abide in Love the Spirit of God's Peace	158
About the Author	161
Reference/Related Readings	163

Living in the Holy Spirit of God's Love

"No one has seen God at any time; if we love one another, God abides in us, and His love is perfected in us." (1 John 4:12) (1)

All are living in the Holy Spirit of God's Love. We then ask, who is God? Where is God? What is God? As I recall from first grade religion, God is Spirit, God is everywhere. God lives in, and as part of, everything. God is everything. This Holy and Divine Spirit is the substance of all that exists. God possess all the qualities of the human soul and yet is an immortal Divine being. God is living in the presence of this moment and eternally in all of creation. Let us be a channel of God's Love, Life, and Peace.

We are living in the Holy Spirit of Divine Love. Only Love is of God because God is Love. Darkness immediately disappears in the moment that a light appears. Darkness and all adversity is absent in the Light of God. All are one; we are individual and yet One in mind in the Spirit of Love. This is the Will of God that is written within our Heart. We pray now for all in our personal and holy family; our sisters, brothers, friends and all in need, for a vision of the Light of Love and Peace.

God is living; there is life that is visible in all of nature. We see the dawn and sunrise of each new day. The earth is precisely and meticulously moving. Life is so intricate and detailed that to deny planned and intelligent purpose in all existence is to say that something just appeared from chaotic substance. God lives in all that is Life. God is energy, which is intelligent, creative spirit and the reason for all of existence. The perfection and detail of every phase of being is divine. God is the universal spirit of all things.

Our mission is Peace and Love for all of creation. God created heaven and earth and all that exists. Enlighten your mind, heart and soul and know that we are one in Love. There is life that is visible in all of nature; "for in Him we live and move and exist." (Hebrews 11:1) (1) God lives in all that is Life. This is a deep mystery that we do not comprehend but must experience and feel the presence of Holy Love. Magnificent beauty and splendor exist. The Stillness of the Mind during silent meditation leads to a vision of Heaven on Earth. God is Love, aware, knowing, conscious of self, personal and yet universal and the eternal creative energy permeating and filling all with Life. This is the spirit of God.

Everything is God and part of God. All that we encounter is mystical and is a natural occurrences or an unexplained reality. Humanity often considers the unexplained mystical. The mysteries of life are scientific facts, waiting to be discovered. According to Scripture, God created humankind in the image and likeness of God. All that we are as human beings God is. If we exist and life exists then God exists and is alive and well. We are co-creators in a universal existence. All that exists is eternal. All things, God formed, using nothing but that which is of the divine nature. Matter, energy, intelligence and thought, desire and creativeness all that we see in our self exists within God. Energy is eternal. It always exists and is indestructible. Matter is a slower moving form of energy. All is of one substance. All creation occurred with in the mind of the universal creator. We have energy so therefore God has energy, we can think therefore God can think. We have life. God has Life. God is living here and now in every move and every breath. God is life and Love, and all things all creation.

We live and move in God's Holy Spirit. God is the energy of life and the way that leads, motivates, and gives us our being. Reality is the manifestation of an object that you see, hear, feel, and believe. We have eyes so we can see and we have ears to hear. Look and listen, God is everywhere and in all things. God is life and the life that is in all things and all of existence. The living God is part of us and lives, moves, and has being in every living creature. God is eternal, and always present. We know as fact that there is life and God is life. All that we experience is an expression of the Divine nature of our Creator who is only good.

The Stillness of the Mind during meditation leads to a vision of Heaven on Earth. God is Love, aware, knowing, conscious of self, personal and yet universal and the eternal creative energy permeating and filling all with Life. All of reality is mystical, and transcendent. According to Scripture, God created humankind in the image and likeness of God. All that we are as human beings God is. If we exist and life exists then God exists. We are co-creators in a universal, eternal, existence. All that we experience is an expression of the Divine nature of our Creator who is only good.

Most religions are faith based, which is belief without absolute knowing. To know something is to take away choice or freewill. This would make us puppets on a string. As a Christian, I have faith in the existence of God the Father, Son, and Holy Spirit. I believe in Jesus who is the Christ, the physical personification of the one God. I believe and I have faith in God of my own free will. This is a gift of freedom that God bestows on humanity. Lack of choice eliminates individuality and our existence as a person. Therefore, absolute knowing eliminates choice and the concept of self as a free and independent individual. I believe, I have faith and I trust. If God suddenly appeared to all people and said; I am here, you can see, hear, touch and feel my presence, and demonstrated proof of this, all would know but without a choice. This would be the end of faith, religion, choice, freewill, and all that makes us human beings. Freedom and the choice to exercise that freedom are the essence of our humanity. We can only love because we are free to love otherwise it would not be love. Believers live by Faith. Life appears as though we are living in a dream. Mankind fell asleep and lost consciousness of our true reality in the presence of God.

Awaken now and the Divine Light will glow in our mind, heart and soul to enlighten our life and thoughts. This is a way of Living in the Spirt of

God. The Divine Light of Holy Love will glow in our mind, heart and soul to enlighten our life and thoughts. This is the way to the Arising Spirt of God on Earth as in Heaven.

Dear God, during Meditative prayer, be our guide for living according to your perfect will. Clear away concern and bestow blessings for health, peace, safety and guidance. There is a need, due to Love, to think of those whom we care for. Guide the way to trust and faith that you, Dear Lord God, are protecting and caring for all people. Bless us and all for whom we pray with your guidance and wisdom to live in Your Holy Spirit of Love. We pray for forgiveness as we forgive. We ask to be free of all that separates us. You are the Lord God who cares for all. Thank you Dear God for all your Love and Blessings. Amen

Living in the Spirit of God
In the Beginning There is Love

Spiritual Care bestowed with kindness, love and compassion leads to Living in the Spirit of God. This is a manifestation here and now of Heaven on Earth. We are evolving toward a level of Higher Consciousness. This leads away from the individual self and extends the mind and soul toward a level of sacred perfection and beauty that is a gift given by the Grace of God. This concept includes multiple interpretations throughout the earth but all are part of One Divine Truth. There are many names but only One God.

Although we are many, we are one in God and yet individual. We are a special and sacred creation with a free will and the purpose of becoming a friend of God. God wants you to be another person to love and care for. This is the reason for your creation. You are given a human soul in order to surrender it freely to the Love of God, your creator. Let your soul, grow in Spiritual oneness with God. Of your own free will, live according to Divine Will. This is essential in order to be able to truly say, "I Love

You and you are mine. I thank you God, I Love You. The way to eliminate selfishness is to say I Love "You". I love you only because you are you. You are who you are created to be. You are my sister, my brother, my child, my Love. You are mine, we are one and I Love you. You are my friend and now we are of one Sacred Spirit.

"In the beginning God created the heavens and the earth. The earth was formless and void, darkness was over the surface of the deep, and the Spirit of God was moving over the surface of the waters. Then God said, "Let there be light"; and there was light. ..." (Genesis 1) (1)

God is Light; "This is the message we have heard from Him and announce to you, that God is Light, and in Him there is no darkness at all."(John 1-5) (1) In the beginning, there was the eternal Spirit of God. Everything that exists is composed using orderly creative energy; this is Sacred Spirit. Science now begins to support the ancient beliefs of eastern teachings that we live in a world of illusion. The physical world in fact is both particle and wave unified into one interacting unit. The concept that we are "light beings" takes on a clearer meaning through this concept. "We are spiritual beings having a human experience". Divine grace and power flows within our mind and soul. This is the Light of God.

Components of Life and Conscious Existence

Energy is the ability to move, create, and work. It is the power moving all things. Energy is the capacity of a physical system to perform work. The reality of energy is that matter (mass) and energy are interchangeable through Einstein's formula, $E=mc2$. Of course this can also be written $m=E/c2$. Matter/mass is equal to energy "slowed down" by the speed of light squared. Matter the substance of physical objects and energy are interchangeable. Matter is that which has weight and occupies space. It is a slower vibration of energy. It occupies space, and is perceivable by one or more physical senses. Matter includes a physical body, a physical substance, or the universe as a whole. According to physics matter may actually be nothing more than a series of organized patterns out of focus and that subatomic "particles" are not really made of energy, but simply are energy. It requires intelligence and creative energy to organize.

Intelligence is the ability to think, reason, know and create in an orderly manner. The ability to attribute mental states to oneself and others and to understand that others have beliefs, desires, and intentions that are different from one's own. Feeling is the ability to be content, to have feelings, emotion, love, and peace. It is the ability to express mental states showing emotion or sensitivity. Synonyms include, sensitive, warm, warmhearted, tender, tenderhearted, caring, sympathetic, kind, compassionate, understanding and thoughtful. Will is the ability to choose and make decisions independently. This is free will which also is a gift that is given to humanity. Will, inspires motivation to accomplish tasks. Free will allows independent decision to choose our course of action.

Energy is eternal. Matter is a slower moving vibrational energy. It is eternal substance, which changes in form. This is God/Transcendent/Divinity/ the Force or Creator. The Spirit of God possesses the power to move and create using intelligence, mind, thought and all the components of life. God created humanity in His own image. We are an extension of God. We are at one. "Then God said, "Let Us make man in our image, according to our likeness; God created man in His own image, in the image of God He created him; male and female He created them." (Genesis 26- 28) (1)

As God extended himself using all creative energy, power, intelligence, will, mind and matter, the Son of God emerged. As the Son, the first extension of God, created of Himself, there arose all souls within a Holy Spirit God. We are living in the Spirit of God this present moment. God possess all power to manifest in many forms and with various names but there is only one universal God. God lives in and through all and yet maintains individuality. This is infinite spirit and personal. God is body, mind, spirit, and soul indicating a separate person and yet at one with all. God is creative loving, kind and only good. God is intelligent aware and possesses all knowledge and wisdom. We know that this is true because we are living examples of that which is now and forever.

The purpose and reason for creation is to live in the Spirit of God as a Friend. We are of our own free will to live according to an infinite plan, a design for perfect living according to one law of Love for God and each other. Separation from this request leads to chaos automatically according to the Divine scheme of creation. We are the creators of our own reality. Our purpose is to maintain order through love and respect for each other and all creation. This is only a small portion of a much greater reality. It is a simple interpretation based upon various spiritual, religious, philosophical teachings and faith. "Everything should be as simple as possible, but no simpler." (Albert Einstein) Spiritual Healing is uncomplicated through faith, trust and belief in this Divine power.

Spiritual Healing of the Whole Self

Healing is an art it is not a science. Medical Care is the art of finding and treating individual needs. Each person is different; therefore healing and method of treatment necessitates an individual plan of care. Healing requires loving care combined with miraculous intervention. A cure is recovery from a disease. It is restoration to physical health. There is however much more involved in recovery from a disease. In order to remedy a problem or illness, the original or fundamental cause is treated. Superficial remedies will not change the condition. They may temporarily alleviate symptoms but unless the whole person including mind, body and soul is included, it is incomplete. Our perception of the problem changes but the potential for re-occurrence still exists. It is necessary to change behavior, environment, beliefs, your mind and soul.

To heal is to make whole and restore health to the highest level of wellness. The actual disease may remain but you are whole. Healing is restoration to health, but the definition of "making whole" is not the same as curing.

Healing focus is on the "wholeness". When we restore someone to a state of wellness, they are not always restored to the original state. The physical disease may or may not disappear but we did help that person.

A person is whole without conquering all illness and discomfort. The separation from fragments of our own soul and God causes problems. Healing brings together the whole person body, mind, soul and Spirit; it restores the normal state. Healing can take place even in the presence of illness. Before we leave this life, there is healing. God's Kingdom is here in the present moment. Healing requires action for change in our life now. There is restoration to a state of wellness through trust, faith and the loving peace that extends from God.

Healing is an important part of life. It is our purpose in this life to heal. Healing makes our life complete. Curing a disease is a partial remedy; our purpose is to restore wholeness. Returning a segment of the physical body to its normal state is important but it is also necessary to remove the original cause of the condition. Restoring to wholeness and a state of wellness is the goal for healing. This requires a change in thinking that leads to self-acceptance, faith and trust.

"There is a river whose streams make glad the city of God, The holy dwelling places of the Most High." (Psalm 46: 4) (1) A place of peace exists within the mind, heart, and soul. Silence your thoughts, clear your mind, remain quiet and rest. This leads toward a pure and serene awareness of existence. This Holy Sanctuary exists when quieting the mind and attuning to the truth of God. Our mind is then clear to receive guidance from the Spirit of God. The Holy Spirit is the source directing us toward reaching our greatest purpose. Awareness of our spiritual nature and connection with God revitalizes our life. Healing, inner peace, happiness and the fulfillment of God's purpose are the result as guidance flows from the Holy Spirit.

"Cease striving and know that I am God; I will be exalted among the nations, I will be exalted in the earth." (Psalm 46: 10) (1) You are aware of God's reality on a spiritual level of consciousness as you quiet your mind and pray. Past, present and future are one and exist in the moment. Life is eternal in God's world. This is a level of consciousness where awareness of your spiritual self creates Inner Peace through faith. Within the realm of God all are of one mind and yet retain an individual personality. There is One God, one sense of spirituality and belief.

Holistic Health Care

Methods of Holistic, Faith based healing include, caring, counseling, education and information. Empathetic, loving care will lead to Inner Peace and Healing of the Whole person. Holistic Health Care involves caring for spiritual, emotional, mental and physical needs. With Loving thought, embrace all who have touched our life. Keep each person close in the sanctity of this present moment and pray with thankful appreciation for the blessings that we share. Dear God Thank You for the Spirit of Your Love that unifies us in a place of Sacred Peace. This is a Holy Alliance that makes life complete.

There is a spiritual method of finding genuine inner peace. Spiritual care leads to the realization of God's Holy purpose. This is achieved when empathy and compassion are the focus. Following is an explanation of the various methods of access to the inner mind leading to inner peace and healing. Meditative Prayer Imagery includes a combination of strategies for personal healing. We find a very real place during this journey into Holy Blessedness. Each view of reality is an individual creation. Now we will begin to build a connection with God's truth.

Managing Stress through Faith

Stress is a natural reaction to an experience that causes a person to feel defenseless or troubled. When we feel threatened whether it is real or imaginary an automatic process known as the "fight-or-flight-or-freeze" reaction also called the stress response occurs. The stress response is the body's method of protection. Its' purpose is to help us to remain focused, energetic, and alert. In emergencies, stress can save a life by giving extra strength to defend our self and others. The stress response also helps an individual to deal with challenges. Stress is what keeps us alert, active and improves concentration. Stress stops being helpful at a point, and starts causing major problems to physical and emotional health, efficiency, interactions, and the quality of life. It is important to learn effective methods of managing stress.

Any change that occurs whether it is good or bad is a form of stress. Change is part of Life. It is important to learn to deal with life situations in a manner that will prevent physical and emotional illness. Stress is a major cause of illness. Managing disorder related to stress requires learning to regulate thoughts and feelings. Relax quiet your mind and listen to what God is telling you. Thoughts create our reality. Good thoughts lead to effective control of feelings. Have Faith and Trust that God is caring for all aspects of life. Trust leads to inner peace and healing. Absolute faith creates miracles.

During stressful situations, learn effective and individual methods of dealing with these events God's Way. Talk to God in prayer. Ask for guidance and help. Always do what is right according to Gods Will and devise a plan of action accordingly. We each have personal needs and problems requiring an appropriate plan. It is important to take into consideration the physical, emotional and mental factors. Use effective methods of self-regulation by learning healthy strategies for dealing with problems and changes. Learn to adapt to each situation that arises by having faith and trust that God is in charge and taking care of us and all whom we love.

Stress can have a positive or negative influence on mental and physical health depending on the methods used when dealing with life issues. Proper methods of stress management will help to meet the challenges of life. Become aware of feelings. Explore the cause of an emotion and then devise a plan or positive action to deal with it. Do all that is possible to solve a problem. Then, relax, have faith and let God be in charge. Stress is a major factor in contributing to the majority of illnesses and injury.

Various relaxation techniques assist in the treatment of Stress related Disorder. Health care professionals recommend mental relaxation combined with appropriate medical treatment, proper nutrition, rest and exercise for individuals with hypertension, heart disease, chronic pain and many other conditions. Seek help from a licensed health care provider. Always continue with prescribed medical treatment. The techniques suggested here are in addition to traditional medical care. Many healthy individuals incorporate the use of various relaxation techniques as a strategy for maintaining health and wellness. Regular practice and determination is important for reaching the desired effect.

Healthy methods of stress management include learning to change thinking patterns. Live in the present moment since reality is now. Understand that the past is over it is therefore not a present reality. The future has not occurred it may never occur it is therefore not a present reality. Treasure beautiful moments from the past and plan for a wonderful future free of worry in the presence of God. Get in touch with feelings and become aware of needs and goals. Start journaling and writing, thoughts, feelings and inspiration. Listen only to that which comes from God who is only good. Deal with problems using effective problem solving strategies. Learn methods of problem solving and take responsibility for personal behavior. Become an expert in methods of relaxation, meditation and prayer. Participate in spiritual, religious and healing groups. Place all things in the hands of God.

The Relaxation Process

Research has revealed that the body chemistry actually changes during a state of deep relaxation. According to medical research, there is a decrease in heart rate, lower blood pressure, changes in skin temperature such as warming of your hands, adjustments in certain types of brain wave activity. The result of this restful state can be monitored using scientific instrumentation. Reactions to resting your mind and body occur instantly as physiological changes, which are monitored using methods of Biofeedback.

Think good thoughts and rest your mind and body, your health and wellbeing depend on it. The relaxation process is very powerful. Rest assured you are the manager of your own life. There is an actual change in brain wave activity. In the course of EEG Biofeedback, we can actually train a person to remain in an Alpha state of relaxation. Alfa is the brainwave that you maintain while resting your mind and thoughts. Theta is a slower brainwave, which leads to a deeper state of relaxation and a higher level of consciousness. Inspiration then flows from the Spirit of God.

One method that may be used is progressive muscle relaxation. Rest in a comfortable position and focus on relaxing each of the muscles of your body. Closing your eyes and imagining yourself in a peaceful place where you are comfortable and at ease is a method of hypnotic induction. Give suggestions to your subconscious mind to work out a solution to a problem without conscious awareness of what is occurring. View within your mind any situation and change it in a way that will resolve the underlying issue. As stated, what your inner mind believes is your reality. Accept what you feel and believe that it is helpful and appropriate or reject anything that you wish. Remember that you are always alert and in control.

Mental Imagery Hypnotic Effect

During a state of restful peace and relaxation, the conscious mind is distracted. The subconscious or inner mind then becomes dominant. This inner mind is more accepting of suggestions and mental images than the conscious mind and believes what it receives to be reality. During this restful state, constructive suggestion in the form of imagery given to the subconscious mind leads to healing from within. By the power of God, mental images cause action for transformation and inner healing. There is the experience of relaxation and physiological changes that lead to an optimistic attitude and an increased sense of well-being. This is a self-hypnotic ability that is helpful in the healing process.

Imaging is the process of creating a specific representation of a desire. When entering a state of relaxation and during imagery or visualization the mind is actively working to accomplish a goal. You are always in control. You decide according to personal belief systems and moral values which images or suggestion to accept or reject. There is an increased susceptibility to suggestion but you must be willing and desire to accept suggestions.

As soon as there is a distraction of the conscious mind, the subconscious mind becomes active. You are always in control and have the ability to reject suggestion or images. The decision as to what you wish to accomplish is always yours. While resting in a peaceful state, you may give yourself personal suggestions. Mental suggestions given to your self should be believable, measurable, focused on the present and given using only positive words.

Imagery is a method of using your imagination to promote relaxation, relieve or cope with symptoms of illness and promote healing. The mind and body function in harmony to improve health. Images received by the subconscious mind are mentally accepted and cause the inner mind to begin to create the realism associated with that image. Mental images created by thought lead to a true vision of the outer reality and actual physical change.

During guided imagery, you visualize a specific goal and clearly image within your mind methods of accomplishing that goal. For instance, cancer patients may visualize the destruction of the cancer cells. Imagery is similar to other relaxation techniques. Guided Imagery is a technique used by health care providers for assisting clients with anything from healing their bodies to solving problems or reducing stress. Guided Imagery with focus on health issues promotes physical and emotional healing.

Imagery includes effective breathing and relaxation techniques. Helpful suggestion leads to constructive change. Imagery induces a very peaceful state of relaxation. It alleviates pain and promotes comfort. Your natural healing response is stimulated leading to improved health and faster healing during illness. Healthy individuals practice imagery to promote and maintain health. You create your reality within the mind. Think good, pleasant thoughts. Image your perfect reality and allow it to happen according to God's perfect will.

In the process of guided relaxation and mental imagery, there is slowing of respiration and normalizing of the heart rate. Therapeutically, this restful state of relaxation and imagery assists in the treatment of many physical and psychological conditions. It helps to enhance the immune system.

Contemplation

St. Thomas Aquinas wrote, "It is requisite for the good of the human community that there should be persons who devote themselves to the life of contemplation." In Christian mysticism, contemplative prayer or contemplation is a form of prayer distinct from spoken prayer and from meditation. In meditation, mind, imagination, and other faculties are involved in an effort to understand our relationship with God.

In contemplative prayer, you decrease this activity so that contemplation has been described as "a gaze of faith", "a silent love"(2) 2724. Contemplative prayer is a form of prayer distinct from spoken prayer and from meditation. In meditation, mind, imagination, and other faculties are involved in an effort to understand our relationship with God. Meditation serves as a foundation on which contemplative prayer begins.

In Teresa's book: The Life of Saint Teresa of Jesus, she says: This spark "seems to ... Rise from the ashes. They shall mount up with wings like eagles, they shall run and not be weary, Teresa says, "You will have read certain books on prayer which advise the soul to enter within itself: and that is exactly what this means." The Rapture of the Soul, Teresa says, "One kind of rapture is this." The soul is yearning for God and He "is moved with compassion". Then, we become like the phoenix that "catches fire and springs into new life." She says, the soul is cleansed and "God unites it with Himself, in a way which none can understand save it and He". (The Interior Castle: Sixth Mansions: Chapter Four) (18)

There is no definite border between Christian meditation and Christian contemplation, and they sometimes coincide.

Saint Teresa of Avila described four degrees or stages of mystical union:

"1. Incomplete mystical union, or the prayer of quiet or supernatural recollection, when the action of God is not strong enough to prevent distractions, and the imagination still retains a certain liberty;

2. Full or semi-ecstatic union, when the strength of the divine action keeps the person fully occupied but the senses continue to act, so that by making an effort, the person can cease from prayer.

3. Ecstatic union, or ecstasy, when communications with the external world are severed or nearly so, and one can no longer at will move from that state.

4. Transforming or deifying union, or spiritual marriage (properly) of the soul with God,

Thus it is that in mystical union we feel God within us and in a very simple way." (Catholic Encyclopedia 1908)

Meditation Defined

Meditation is a way of clearing mind and body of all that delays the Creative Spirit of God from entering. Sacred Power flows through the subtle spiritual centers of the body. Meditation is attuning our mental and physical body to God. It is bonding and connecting with the Holy Spirit. Preparation is necessary for meditation. We clear away the cares of the world and strive to be a Living Temple of the Holy Spirit. Reach for purity of mind body and soul and await the presence of the Lord God. This is the art of learning to quiet our thoughts and clear our mind. It is a state of increased awareness in a union with God.

There is perception and clarity of the mind, while decreasing intentional mental thought. It is the ability to direct attention to a place of silence and peace. We focus thoughts away from all worry or concern and remain in the present moment with God. Inner guidance, heightened awareness and a higher level of consciousness exists. Prayer is talking to God, asking a question and requesting an answer. Meditation is silently waiting and listening for an answer. The answers flow from God's Holy Spirit of intelligence, wisdom and truth leading to an elevation in spiritual awareness, ultimate peace and mental calmness. There is a healing effect on the body, mind and soul.

Preparing for Meditative Prayer

We prepare our mind, body and soul to reach a place of silent meditation and contemplation through meditative prayer. Each Meditative Prayer Imagery will lead us closer to that place where we are ready to receive the Holy Spirit of God as our guest. This is where we clear away the cares of the world and strive to be a Living Temple of the Holy Spirit. Reach for purity of mind body and soul and await the presence of the Lord God. We are always together and abide in Love which is the Spirit of God's Sacred Peace.

Prepare by resting in a comfortable position free of disturbance. Close your eyes and focus on your breathing. Slow controlled breaths cause immediate relaxation. Consciously relax your muscles especially around your face, jaw, neck and shoulders. Create within your mind an attitude of willingness to accept the guidance that you receive. Begin with prayer and request guidance then quietly wait for an answer as you focus on a sound, word or peaceful music. Understand that if you asked a question the only way to receive an answer is to listen quietly. As thoughts come into your mind just let them float by like leaves on a peaceful stream.

This soothing state of awareness enhances and hastens the healing process. Entering a state of meditative prayer prepares our mind for acceptance of information that leads to the desired change. The mind becomes receptive to new and revitalizing inspiration. It is similar to clearing a writing board to supply space for new information. This is a method of instilling peace, order and infinite love into one's life. Meditative prayer is a preliminary step in the process of learning to regulate and control mental and physical functioning. It is a doorway to the inner mind leading to God.

Centering Prayer

Centering is also a method of quieting our mind and listening to the Divine inspiration that flows from the Holy Spirit of God. This leads to a state of contemplation which is contemplative prayer. This is the ultimate purpose in all methods of meditative prayer. Always begin any form of meditation with prayer. Sit in a comfortable position and relax by using any of the methods of quieting the mind and body previously stated and the meditative prayer imagery prescriptions to follow. When you are sitting and relaxed choose a sacred word or phrase and repeat this word in your mind. When thoughts come into your mind, let them move by peacefully and continue to focus on your word or phrase. Continue this for as long as you are comfortable and then let yourself rest in the silence and peace of God's Love. Thank God for this Blessing. (10)

Divine Reading

Lectio Davina, the Latin for "Divine Reading", is the practice of scriptural reading, meditation and prayer intended to promote communion with God and to increase the knowledge of God's Word. We read scripture slowly as the Living Word rather than focus on the text. Lectio Davina includes four separate steps: read; meditate; pray; contemplate. A passage of Scripture is read, then we reflect upon the reading. This is followed by prayer and contemplation on the Word of God. Theological analysis is avoided. Higher Christ Consciousness provides meaning.

Christian Meditation

According to Christian Doctrine, prayer begins with vocal prayer, then moves on to a more structured form in terms of Christian meditation, and finally reaches the deep levels of contemplative prayer. Contemplative prayer follows Christian meditation and is the highest form of prayer that aims to achieve a close spiritual union with God. Christian teachings have emphasized the use of meditative prayers as an element in increasing one's knowledge of Christ.

Meditative Prayer Imagery

Meditative prayer imagery is a combination of methods of prayer that will help to restore mental, physical and spiritual health. Meditative prayer creates a specific state of mind that leads to acceptance of inner guidance from God's Holy Spirit. Focused forming of Holy and scriptural mental images are used for inspiration. The methods presented in the following meditative prayer imagery are a combination of techniques that will enhance the healing process. Meditative imagery includes prayer, relaxation and focusing on peaceful imagery which produces a very peaceful state of mind and body,

Meditative Imagery and prayer supports an atmosphere for healing. This is a method of instilling inner peace and healing. Included are suggestions for healing of mind and body. You may include individual suggestions according to personal needs. When using Meditative Prayer Imagery for self-help, read each section slowly then close your eyes, rest in a comfortable position and perform the techniques for relaxation of mind and body. There is an automatic relaxation effect while reading. It is also helpful to record the imagery and rest as you listen. Play soft soothing music to enhance the effect. Always focus on good uplifting thoughts. Start from the beginning and progress toward your greatest desire.

Creating a Prescription for Spiritual Healing

Always begin with prayer. Ask God's Holy Spirit to Guide and protect. Only good is of God. State, "Only good, loving, thoughts, ideas and feelings will influence you in any way." Everyone is spiritual and motivated by their individual beliefs even those who are non-religious. Spirituality is important in the healing process. Decide on a plan of action together. In order to help another person, it must be what he or she wishes to accomplish. Focus only on Goodness, healing and Love.

There are specific guidelines for writing imagery scripts for yourself or others. Only clear positive statements are used. Remain in the present tense. State in simple sentences what to wish to accomplish. An example is "You are peaceful and calm." You are a healthy and beautiful child of God. "God loves you and wants you to feel good, and joyful. Avoid using words that have a double or multiple meaning and any negative words; think of how you would like to feel and state it clearly and specifically. "You are healing as it is God's perfect will." Only Good is of God; the Holy Light of God is filling your mind, body and soul with the divine spirit of Healing and peace.

Avoid the words "no", "you will not ", not" any more"; always focus on what you will do. These words are unacceptable to the inner mind and you will obtain the opposite result. The only reality is the present moment. When speaking to a patient or client assess their situation, beliefs, and spirituality, motivation and health issues. Use sentences that will motivate beneficial changes. Use language according to the person's intelligence and age level. Use a slow calm, peaceful voice. Be caring empathetic and compassionate. Also avoid the word" try". The inner mind interprets this word as "attempt but don't do it."

Health Care providers develop a plan of care based on the following. Collect data; this includes information related to immediate needs, anticipated needs and the present situation. This includes holistic spiritual beliefs and practices. Assess the situation based upon all the information that you gather though talking, known health concerns and medical diagnosis. Plan, with the person you are assisting, methods of resolving problems and caring for needs. Develop specific short term and long-term goals to be accomplished within a specific time. Before meditative prayer, learn to relax.

Prescription for Relaxation

In preparation for meditation and inner healing, rest and clear your mind. Always begin with silent prayer. Within your mind, request guidance, and envision your body shielded and protected by God's Heavenly Light. Only positive loving thoughts or feelings will influence you in any way. A shield of God's Divine Power surrounds and protects you. You are in total control. You may change any thought in accordance with your present needs. Positive thought leads to positive action. Now you are relaxing completely, just rest in the silence.

Breathe in deeply and exhale slowly three or four times and then continue to breathe normally. As you breathe become aware of your abdominal area rising and falling. Rest, close your eyes and sense a vibration as you relax each muscle. Become aware of any tightness and then just let it go. Start at top of your head; sense a soothing vibration flowing gently. Let all your facial muscles relax. Let your eyes relax, your nose, your mouth, and your jaw. Now let your neck relax completely. Feel the muscles in your neck becoming loose and comfortable and let that soothing sensation spread into your shoulders. Feel your shoulders relaxing completely. Just let your shoulders drop down as you begin to drift and rest.

Now rest your arms at your side and focus on your hands feeling warm and tingling right into your fingers. Become aware of this gentle, soothing, feeling moving into your chest ... your abdominal area your hips, your legs, your knees, your ankles and your feet. Breathe in deeply and exhale slowly. Imagine that a tranquilizing vapor is filling the air. With each breath, you are becoming more peaceful and calm. You are always in complete control. You may do whatever you wish to ensure that you are comfortable. As you rest there, your inner mind is aware of all that is occurring. During this or any relaxation only good, pleasant thoughts, ideas or feelings will influence you in any way.

Meditative Prayer Imagery Prescriptions

The following meditative prayer prescriptions are written with the intension of promoting inner peace and healing. Pray for peace, guidance and God's protection prior to each meditative prayer. Rest your mind and body using preliminary relaxation techniques and proceed with the meditative prayer imagery prescription.

Steps to Meditative Prayer and Holy Presence Include:

1. Spoken and Mental Prayer for Guidance and the Holy Presence of God

2. Focus, Relaxation, Imagery, Visualization for promoting peace and leading to a peaceful mind.

3. Silence, and Contemplation to quiet and clear your mind of all thought

4. Receive Inspiration and Guidance from God to help yourself and others

Prepare to Relax

Do whatever is necessary to avoid disturbance. Be sure that phones are off. Rest in a comfortable position. Rest your hands on your lap with palms turned upward if comfortable for you. During Meditative prayer you are in a fully relaxed and peaceful state and yet awake and aware of all that is occurring. You are always in control of your thoughts and feelings. If needed, do whatever you require to remain comfortable and return to the meditation. Now you will experience a very peaceful and sacred place

Focus Only on the Good

Meditative Prayer is a method of instilling peace, order and infinite love into your life. "Meditate in your heart, and be still." May the Light of God, guide you, protect you and lead you as you enter God's Holy Place of Peace and Love. Meditative prayer leads to a quiet mind and focus on the present moment. Inner guidance flows from God's Holy Presence. Only good is from God. Darkness can never exist in the Light of God. Accept only peaceful, loving thoughts and feelings. Always be aware and discerning. Immediately change and eliminate any uncomfortable thought or feeling. Pray: "Light of God, Spirit of God be my guide let only your peace and Love influence me in any way,"

Begin with Prayer

Dear God, may the light of your Holy Spirit fill us, surround, guide, and protect as we enter into Your Holy place of peace, goodness and love. Guide us on this path of spiritual growth and bring us closer to you. Our Lord, God we ask you to always be our guide. As we open our mind and heart to You Lord God, help us to listen, so that we hear your voice, and let your word flow into our mind and soul. Fill us with your Holy Spirit, and let the light of your infinite love, peace and inner healing enter our mind, heart, soul and life. Bless all for whom we pray. Give us faith to believe that all who we know and love are safely in your care. Bless us with your gift of grace and faith that we may live in accord with your will. Help us to understand and to believe that only goodness is of you. We thank you God for all your Blessings.

Rest in the Presence of God

Relax all your facial muscles; let your jaw drop down and relax. Let all the muscles in your neck relax, and let your shoulders relax and drop down. Rest your arms in a comfortable position. Receive God's Holy Light. Become aware of a peaceful sensation throughout your entire being. Always be mindful of the Holy Presence of God with you to guide and care for you.

In the Hands of God

Let the future go and place it in the Hands of God.

Place all your loved ones in the Hands of God.

Place yourself in the Hands of God.

When we place all in the Hands of God, a transformation occurs.

Any event affecting loved ones and yourself transforms into growth, understanding, healing and inner peace. Release any concern, have trust and faith, knowing that God is in charge.

By letting go and having faith in God's plan, you find a place of harmony and inner peace. You are strengthened and renewed.

As you have faith and put yourself in the Hands of God, attitudes and beliefs lead you toward your highest good. You are opening the way for complete peace and joy to fill your life.

Only the goodness of God will influence you in any way. You are safe, secure and completely sheltered by God's Holy Presence. The Light of God is enfolding, protecting, and guiding you. Now this journey is going to lead you to your special place of serenity and healing

1. Ascending in the Holy Spirit

The Holy Spirit bestows gifts that lead to the presence of God and a higher level of Consciousness. Prayer prepares us to enter God's place of peace and Holy Silence. A quiet mind and subdued thought leads to guidance from God's Holy Spirit. This is an assent into a sacred level of consciousness. You communicate clearly within your mind and spirit. Body, mind, and soul merge in an environment of blessed goodness.

Wisdom is the first and main gift of the Holy Spirit. It is the fulfillment of the spiritual virtue of faith. Through wisdom, you learn to appreciate the doctrines that we believe through faith. The truths of Spiritual belief are greater than the possessions of this world. Wisdom enlightens you to understand your connection with God's Creation.

Understanding is the second gift of the Holy Spirit. Wisdom is the aspiration to contemplate God; understanding gives you the ability to comprehend, to a limited extent, the very substance of the truths of Faith. Through understanding, we move beyond faith.

Counsel, the third gift of the Holy Spirit, is the fulfillment of the essential virtue of prudence or judgment. Prudence is a practice used by many but counsel is mystical. You are able to judge how to act properly almost by intuition or foresight. Because of the gift of counsel, you have the courage to proclaim the truth of the Faith, because the Holy Spirit will guide you in defending those truths.

Fortitude is the fourth gift of the Holy Spirit. Fortitude gives you the strength to follow through on the actions learned through the gift of counsel. It is courage, but it goes beyond courage. Fortitude is the virtue of the martyrs that allowed them to die rather than to renounce the Faith.

Knowledge is the fifth gift of the Holy Spirit. It is similar to wisdom. Knowledge is the perfection of faith. Wisdom gives us the desire to judge all things according to the truths of Faith but knowledge is the actual ability to do so. You are able to see the circumstances of your life the way that God sees them. Through this gift of the Holy Spirit, you have the ability to determine God's purpose for your life and live appropriately.

Piety, the sixth gift of the Holy Spirit, is the commitment to worship and to serve God. You then wish to worship God and to serve Him out of love.

Fear of the Lord is the seventh gift of the Holy Spirit. The term fear is to indicate respect, awe and concern. It is a sign of reverence. "The fear of the Lord is the beginning of knowledge; Fools despise wisdom and instruction."(Proverbs 1:6-8) (1) Fear of the Lord confirms the doctrinal virtue of hope. This gift of the Holy Spirit gives the aspiration and the assurance that God will provide us with the grace to keep from offending Him. Our desire not to offend God is more than simply a sense of obligation like piety, the fear of the Lord ascends out of love. (2)

The Holy Spirit of God helps us to understand mystical principles and values. God's eternal flow of spirit creates unity and harmony for all. Now due to individual foresight, we will see God's true light. One who receives the gifts of the Holy Spirit extends to others care and true compassion. Our heart is full of love and concern as we realize the presence of God.

God is the Spirit that gives life to all things; God is loving, caring and possesses all wisdom and intelligence. This is true because it is obviously there for all to see. There is general knowledge that we are intelligent beings with the ability to create, love and care. The source of these realities is God who is infinite, intelligent and creative. This is the Holy Spirit of God acting in our life.

Contemplation leads to a place of peace and awareness of our connection with God who is the foundation of all goodness in creation. As we quiet our mind in meditative prayer, there is increased insight. A quiet mind has the capacity for listening to inner guidance. We then hear the guidance that flows from the Holy Spirit. Listen closely as you subdue your thoughts. A silent mind is a receiver of Holy guidance from the Spirit of God.

Reception of Spiritual Gifts for Healing the Soul

Dear God I ask for guidance according to Your perfect will. As I request Spiritual gifts for Healing of my soul, fill me with Your Holy Spirit of peace, love, and Holy guidance. Let only that which is of your Holy Light influence me in any way. As I pray and meditate on your word. Surround, protect and fill me with your Sacred Healing Light.

Rest in a quiet peaceful location, in a comfortable position, relaxing all your muscles, and start your journey to a place of harmony. Imagine that you are in a place that is comforting and peaceful for you. This is a spiritual dwelling where you are secure and protected by God's Holy Spirit. God is only good. As you rest in this Sanctified place of peace and beauty, begin to feel a sense of harmony. Notice and become aware a Holy Presence surrounding, guiding and filling your mind body and soul. It is as though you are in the presence of Love. You feel loved and cared for. Experience a mild vibration throughout your body and a loving presence.

Sense your connection with God and become aware of total silence as though time suddenly stopped. There is the experience of all existing in the present moment. You are aware only of the present as you rest and accept the guidance that you receive from God's Holy Spirit. Only good will influences you in any way. You are safe, secure and completely protected.

This is your special place in the presence of God leading to reception of God's spiritual gifts. Rest and focus on Holy Light entering your body. Visualize and feel a gentle vibration throughout your body. Create within your mind an appearance of Holy Spiritual Light around yourself. As this flow of Holy Spirit surrounds and fills your entire being, let your inner self join with the Holy Light of God. A gentle loving sensation transfers a feeling of connection with the Spirit of God. Now as the light flows throughout your entire being, become aware of a sacred awareness of stillness.

Breathe deeply and slowly and observe your breathing. With each breath become aware of the Light of God. This Holy Spirit of God is flowing peacefully throughout your entire being. Now you are receiving the healing Love of God. Continue to sense and visualize this pure light entering your body as it flows from the Spirit of God. As the light enters and surrounds your body, sense a silent peaceful state of mind. There is a feeling of security, peace and healing as you rest in the Holy Peace of God.

Your inner sacred awareness is increasing. Experience the silence within your mind. You are in a quiet place of Love and God's Light. You are in that still silent place of God's perfect love. Let go now and rest quietly in the stillness of your mind where all are one. Your mind is quiet, in tune with God and ready to receive inner Holy blessings from God's Holy Spirit. Be still, sense the silence and receive God's Spiritual Gifts.

Ascending in the Spirit of God

As an expression of God's Holy Love, you are provided with strength and vitality as Divine Spirit surrounds protects and fills you with the Healing Light of God. Centering on healing thoughts, we ask God to create a blessing of peace.

Let all the muscles in your face rest, feel each muscle relaxing completely. Rest your eyes, your nose, your cheeks and your jaw. Let your jaw drop down and be sure that your teeth a not clenched together. Allow your neck to relax completely in a restful position. Let your shoulders drop down and relax completely. Focus on a sense of complete relaxation moving throughout your body from the top of your head to the bottom of your feet.

As you rest there, allow the Holy Light of God to ascend throughout your entire being. Begin at the base of your spine, focus your attention on the base of your spine and sense a vibration in this area. Through the Grace of God, you are aware of God's Holy Light moving through your entire being. This is Holy Light, the Light of God.

Abide in Love the Sacred Presence of God

Experience now this vibration in the center of your abdominal area and notice a sense of warmth, peace and God Light at the center of your body. Let that light now ascend upward toward your Heart where you know the Love, Peace, and forgiveness of God. In this place there is only God's Love. You forgive and are forgiven. Let the Light now move to the area of your throat where you sense the presence of God's Holy Word. Become aware of the Healing Light of God. There is complete peace and rest as your focus moves to the center of your forehead where you know and experience all in the clear Light of God. This is a place of spiritual sight and clear vision.

Now let the light move to the crown of your head. With your eyes remaining closed, look up within your mind toward the top of your head. Imagine the ascended light within your mind flowing through the crown of your head and connecting with the Holy Light of God. Let that light extend now to completely encircle your body and reenter at the base of your spine. Create a circle of Holy God Light around your entire being.

As you connect with the Holy Light of God, you are completely surrounded and filled with the Light. With loving concern and care, the Holy Light of God by the power the Holy Spirit heals every part of your body, mind and soul. God's healing light is moving in and through you in a perfect way. As you receive this Holy Light with prayerful awareness, you are creating a healing vibration that moves through your body and functions in a manner that supports your total well-being. As an expression of God's Holy Spirit of eternal life, know that this Spirit of restorative power is moving throughout your entire being.

By the power of God, you are healing in God's perfect way and as it is His perfect will. Amen. Silence your mind now and allow God to help you according to Sacred Holy Divine Will. I thank you Dear God, my Love, my Friend, Protector and Healer

2. Entrance to God's Holy Place of Peace

Within the silence of the mind we find a special place of inner peace where there is clarity in regard to our Divine and Holy purpose in living. In God's Holy place of peace each person is an eternal being created by God. We have faith and trust in the presence of Divine Holiness. God gives life and the ability to be conscious of living, moving, thinking, building and creating. God is the reason for Life and Love. All are one with God Who loves and cares for each soul and form of life. Now we see dimly but all will awaken from this dream of life and return to God's Holy place of peace where we will truly know God and self.

During Meditative Prayer Imagery, we focus on peace and love that leads us closer to sacred spiritual understanding. This occurs as we accept Holy guidance that leads to health and mental peace. Within this special peaceful place, all unite within the Spirit of God. It is a state of unlimited wisdom, knowledge and goodness. This is the spirit of life, which leads to whole person healing. There is guidance from God's Holy Spirit to see and understand. Upon entrance to God's Holy Place of peace, we find complete contentment. Sacred direction transpires as we learn to see and envision the path that God has prepared. Images progress into actuality and inner healing occurs through faith and trust in God.

In sacred prayer we ask God to heal, and guide us toward a place of peace and silence. There is the ability to renew a situation within the mind knowing that the Holy Spirit of God is there to help, heal, guide and protect. Now there is the ability to accept the healing power of God. Mind, soul and body are healing and function in perfect order as we pray. This is possible through the power of God. Thoughts cause feelings that create awareness and beliefs. They determine what we believe to be reality. It is essential to always remain focused on the goodness and peace of God. Pray and allow only focus on healing thought with the help of God.

We are never alone. God is always waiting to help and guide us. There is a sanctuary for finding Inner Peace. This is an entrance to God's Holy Place of Peace. Through the guidance of God's Holy Spirit, enter using our God given ability to create within our mind. Pray for peace and Holy inspiration. Awareness is increased leading to foresight and understanding. The mind is more attentive and discerning of circumstances. Enter this place of sanctity and understanding that exists within the Spirit of God. We have the ability to renew beliefs that can change our concept of living, as we reflect inward and image God's beautiful reality.

During Meditative Prayer Imagery, we enter a peaceful state of mind where there is awareness of a place that is just between being awake and sleeping. This is a spiritual dimension where inspiration is received from the Spirit of God. In this peaceful state, we become mindful that there is a reality beyond this physical realm. The practice of meditative prayer is a form of interaction in a spiritual domain. Enter this Holy Place of Peace with the intention of receiving insight and guidance from the Spirit of God. Always be discerning and know that God is only good. Clear your mind and focus only on that which is of God who is goodness and Love. Imagine that you just asked a question and are silently waiting for an answer. This is an entrance to God's Holy place. It is where we pursue responses to any request. Now begin to comprehend this reality within the Holy Spirit of God. The stillness creates heaven and limitless serenity.

Meditative Prayer Imagery leads to the Holy Presence of God. Use distinctive inner vision and guidance from the Holy Spirit to find the way. Remember that while you are in a relaxed meditative state of prayer that you are always in complete control. You can change any situation by the power of your thought and the help of God. Focus only on good uplifting inspiration, ideas or guidance that flows from the Holy Spirit of God.

Passage to Stillness for Healing the Mind

Dear Lord God, be my guide and protector of my mind heart and soul as I pray and meditate. Lead me to a state of mind that is peaceful and receptive to your Holy Will. Guide my thoughts actions and feelings. As I listen for your voice, let only your Holy Word influence me in any way. Be with me always to help, heal, guide and protect. I thank you Lord.

This imagery is now going to lead you to a place of inner peace and stillness within your mind. This is a place of goodness and comfort leading to inner healing. It is an Entrance to God's Holy Place of Divine order. Attune your mind and thoughts with the Holy Will of God and know that all is in perfect order. As you rest in a comfortable position, close your eyes and begin by focusing on your breathing. Take a deep breath and feel a flow of air moving and spreading peace throughout your body. Take another deep breath, and exhale. Now allow yourself to breathe comfortably. Each time that you breathe, imagine a soothing wave of Holy Light flowing throughout your mind, soul and body.

With each breath, begin to experience a sense of mental clarity. Begin to understand that all knowledge flows from the perfect mind of God. Now, with your eyes closed, look up within your mind, toward the top of your head. See, within your mind a pure light flowing into your body from the top of your head and circulating throughout your body. Avoid thought just rest and allow a flow of holy peace and wisdom to enter.

Quiet your mind for a moment of all thought. As thoughts come into your mind, just let them pass like gently ripples on a stream of moving water. You are feeling a sense of clarity and Holy purpose in all of existence. Breathe in deeply and exhale slowly. Focus on the presence of God's Holy Light within your mind and soul. As your mind and body becomes peaceful, you have the ability to think clearly and make correct decisions according to the perfect will of God. You receive guidance from the Holy Spirit of God to understand all situations according to God's Divine and Sacred purpose.

You are entering a state of complete serenity and stillness within your mind. This is a place of balance and calm. It is where you see and understand clearly, as you connect with the Light of God. Contentment is a state of mind. You control your thoughts and thinking; therefore you control your feelings. Within your mind, request guidance and know that as you are resting, only good, helpful, thoughts and feelings will influence you in any way. Feel yourself entering a very peaceful state of physical and mental rest. Mentally surround yourself with God's Holy Light. You are in total control and influenced only by pleasant helpful thoughts and feelings.

Breathe in deeply and exhale slowly. With each breath, become more secure and accepting of Holy guidance. Imagine the peace of God filling your mind and guiding you in any situation. Continue to rest your mind and experience a place of complete peace and understanding. Now visualize yourself moving through a mist that leads to enlightenment and Holy Peace of Mind and Soul. Your path is reflecting the light of the rising sun. It is so pleasant to sense the peace that flows from the mind of God and feel secure that this Holy Peace is always there for you. The way is through faith and trust that the Holy Spirit of God is here, now and always in the silence of this present moment with God.

Just continue to become more peaceful as you continue to rest and go deeper into a very peaceful state of consciousness. Your awareness increases as you rest and clear your mind. With Divine guidance of God's Holy Spirit, your inner mind is working to resolve any problem. In this place, God has the power to accomplish anything according to His perfect will. God is only good and gives only good and perfect gifts. You are a beloved child of the Creator. Return to God's Holy Place of peace at any time by just closing your eyes and becoming aware of God's Holy Light entering your mind and body. Rest there in the present moment and in the silence of your mind where we find God.

3. The Spirit of Renewed Life

"And do not be conformed to this world, but be transformed by the renewing of your mind, so that you may prove what the will of God is, that which is good and acceptable and perfect" (Romans 12:2) (1)

Each person is a perfect and beautiful creation of the Living God. The human soul and spiritual being is eternal. A soul created to be a companion of the creator and a child of God, with complete trust freely enters this life. Living in this physical form gives an opportunity for experiencing new and wondrous aspects of this Holy Creation. Each person is a Spiritual Being who is living within a physical body. It is important to provide spiritual care for peace and healing of the whole self.

Renewal leads to being secure, peaceful and protected within the Hands of God. All needs are satisfied. There is comfort and security combined with knowledge and the ability of the soul to be mentally and spiritually free. This is a sacred and joyful event as we transform and renew our life.

During Meditative prayer imagery, we journey to into a silent stream of consciousness; this is a place within the mind where a gradual enlightening and transforming occurs.

Renewal of the Spiritual Self

Become aware of your Spiritual Self and move closer to God's Holy Spirit. During preliminary prayer, ask God to help and forgive you. Pray for guidance and trust that the Holy Spirit of God is with you to fill your mind and soul with Holy Light. Forgive all transgression in your life including yourself and others and ask that the Light of Christ, the light of God be with you now and eternally.

Dear God, Let your Holy Spirit of Love and Healing renew my mind, body, and soul. Create within me a channel of help and blessing to all who I know and love. Fill me with Your Spirit of Peace that I may extend your peace and Healing to all in need. Guide me toward renewal of my Spiritual being that I may live in your Holy Light. Be with me to guide and protect and I pray and always. Thank you God for all your blessings

You are now going to use Meditative Prayer imagery to create within your mind a sense of renewed sanctity, beauty and order to transform your mind, soul and spiritual being. This promotes peace and inner healing. Clear your mind of thought. Image yourself, secure and protected by God's Light. Only good exists. You are in total control of your thoughts and feelings. You have God given freedom to transform your thought into harmony.

Breathe in deeply. Breathe out, and let the air move causing a flow of relaxation throughout your body. Now continue to breathe slowly in this manner. Focus on the Light of God and feel Spiritual light moving as it advances through the center of your body and encircles your entire being forming a glowing aura. Continue to focus, calmly avoiding all other thought.

Image a reflection of God's Holy Light guiding you and lighting the way to awareness of your entrance into this sacred reality. Rest and envision yourself, entering your special place where you are peaceful and secure. Clear your mind of all thought and sense the presence of infinite love. As you gaze into the distance, a flash of violet light appears and fills the surrounding area. This light is surrounding you, protecting, purifying and relaxing your mind, body and soul. An awareness of divine protection becomes evident. Sense a presence of loving kindness.

A design for your transformed life becomes evident as you visualize vibrant lights of infinite color and form. The light is constantly changing and reforming. The center is round and glowing. It is in constant motion composing intricate schemes of color and light. As you gaze into the center, there is a gentle sensation of movement forward. Like a magnet, attracting you forward where there is a sense of loving acceptance.

Your spiritual growth is steady and planned by the boundless intelligence of God. The complexity of your life pattern is part of God's infinite order and beauty. Each atom and molecule is a flawless structure of life. You are a new and perfect formation containing all the ingredients needed for Spiritual growth. God's perfect plan of existence is there eternally and totally.

You are a creation of love and beauty formed in the image of the Creator. There is consciousness of self as a unique and perfect being. You are aware of life and naturally realize that it is a gift to cherish. Your spiritual being is unique. You are the result of beauty and perfection in the process of creation. It is all that there is joined in eternal spirit. You are spiritually reborn.

Renewal of your Spiritual self continues in a place of sanctuary and serenity. You receive love and blessings by the Holy Spirit of God. This intricate formation continues as your soul essence performs the task of Spiritual rebirth in a new and unblemished child of God. Your perfection is unique. You are new, refreshed and vibrant in this pattern of living in the Spirit of God. Now you have the ability to sense and feel life and love. You feel loved and cared for. You understand that there is concern for your well-being. Satisfaction is complete and lasting. By the Grace of God, you receive all that you need.

Your mind now begins to focus on the Light of God. Move toward a brilliant center of Holy God Light; as the Spiritual Light of God continues to create its geometric patterns of being. A steady and increasingly powerful movement becomes evident. You move gently and with a sense of security toward a glowing Holy Light. The flow and movement is secure and peaceful. Complete confidence in the purpose of this journey is clear. There is a movement forward into the light and you are spiritually reborn and renewed in the Light of God.

The presence of the Life of God is now evident. Eternal mind, spirit, and matter are merging in a pattern of uniqueness and perfection. You emerge from the center of Holy brilliance and move into the form and spirit of an eternal being. You connect in a bond, which fills you with Holy Love, Peace, and Inner Healing. You have the ability to magnify and see with clarity each new being, flower, tree and all forms of life. There is a sense of merging with all in a sea of oneness and all infinite love. A feeling of closeness and love is evident as the sensation of affection, devotion and loving care becomes apparent. You sense a touch of life and are reborn in an atmosphere of love.

Rest in the Silence now and when you are ready, return with knowledge and understanding of the miracle of this process of Spiritual birth into an atmosphere of peace and eternal love. You are a child of God. You are a child of Goodness. The Breath for Life Eternal fills you as you awaken in the light of this new and perfect day.

4. Healing of the Heart

The Heart automatically responds to life situations that involve emotion. It speeds up during times of stress and slows down during moments of peace. The heart is sensitive to each occurrence during the course of living. We know within our heart the consequences of an emotional issue. Love nurtures and feeds. Anger and hate are destructive forces that cause injury to the heart and all body systems.

In the beginning of life a certain feeling of love exists which creates a natural desire to live with a sense of self-assurance. There is a reason for living that fulfills your natural need for relationships and closeness. There is a feeling of belonging and fulfillment. Closeness to another and the sense of love are fundamental essentials of physical and spiritual growth. A loving touch, caring and gentleness is an essential part of being.

Nurturing with love and kindness, leads to transformation into the light of new life. This is the result of unconditional loving care of the spiritual self. The dependability of warm and kind interaction, combined with the experience of supportive care, convert strain into contentment and peace. The Holy unconditional of Love of God creates a bond of limitless affection that you receive and extend to others. Your heart is then peaceful and maintains an appropriate rhythm. This is a touch of Love and it is a touch of life. This sacred experience involves the combined love of humanity with the joy that is evident in spiritual love. First, establish trust in God, and then extend this spiritual care to others. There are various restorative methods to facilitate spiritual care for inner healing of the heart.

A purpose of life is to understand our oneness with all creation, which gives the ability to live in harmony with all. A sensation of the Holy Love of God is the energy that fills and enlivens each atom and cell of our being as we approach a level of higher consciousness. Whether in the physical, mental or spiritual body, there is the Holy Light of God with us, and then warmth and comfort in the knowledge of unity with all life.

During meditation we learn methods of relaxation for mental peace that will allow the spiritual self to connect with the universal consciousness. There is an actual measurable change in all vital signs of the body that confirm this peaceful state. There is a gentle flow of Loving Spirit. It is like waves in an ocean of warm fluid that projects love and protection, merging all into one. In this bonding of love, you are in touch with sacred creation. There is understanding that gives meaning to life. We experience the presence of God and the joy of feeling love, happiness and peace. It is an awakening in which all was vague, and now the beauty of life is apparent.

The fulfilling love of God is a spiritual blessing that heals our heart, mind, and soul. Sacred Love is the motivation for giving and receiving kindness, compassion and spiritual care of the heart. You are a creation of love and goodness. There is consciousness of self as a distinctive and perfect being that is aware of life and naturally understands its quest to extend God's Holy Love. Sacred awakening of your mind, heart and soul is a unique blessing. You are a perfect creation united within the Heart of the Holy Spirit.

The heart which is the emotional center of feeling maintains timeless memory. The love in our heart is eternal. Memory and impressions within the mind, heart and soul contain the genetic structure, shape and mold an individual personality. This vital creative, intelligent energy of God forms the soul pattern. The image of the human being is unlimited within the Spirit of God. Necessary loving spiritual care is vital for maintaining health and healing of the whole person. Now we are going to transform feelings within the mind. Love and nurturing is there for all to receive within the loving hands of our spiritual parents always living within the mind and heart. During Meditative Prayer, experience yourself, created with intricate order, perfection and sacred Love. Now begin with prayer and the reception of Holy Guidance to bring healing love into the heart of your inner child at commencement of life.

Unconditional Love for Healing of the Heart

Dear God, Be my guide, as I pray and meditate help me to understand and experience your holy presence in a place of unconditional Holy Love. Walk with me on this path toward healing and peace. As I listen quietly, help me to hear your voice and accept your sacred Word. Teach me to love unconditionally that I may receive and extend your Blessings to all who I know and love. I thank you God.

Now begin to rest your mind and body in a comfortable position. Relax all your muscles starting with your facial muscles and continuing to the bottom of your feet. Imagine that you are resting outdoors on a beautiful warm and pleasant day. As you continue breathing normally, feel a comforting wave of lightness as though you are gently floating in a small boat along a peaceful lake, on a clear and pleasant day. A shield of Holy Light surrounds you; as the Spirit of God provides complete protection. You are always safe and secure. Breathe in deeply and exhale slowly. Become aware of the freshness of the air that you breathe, and the soothing sent of nature. With each breath, rest your mind and body. Let your thoughts flow as the ripples on a calm moving stream. Become more rested, as you allow yourself to drift along the flowing water of the lake.

Only pleasant thoughts ideas and feelings can be of any influence. The Divine loving and guiding presence of God is protecting you. Clear your mind of all thought and let yourself receive inner guidance. Love is a feeling that you receive only as a gift of God. The only way to experience Love is to allow only kind and loving sensation to enter your mind and then to interact with others always in a loving way. Be kind, caring, understanding, and compassionate. As you Love others, you receive love in return by the other and by God.

You are entering a place of silence. This is a place of infinite love and peace. Only good exists. Everything is right now in this joyful moment. This is a place of creation. It is a place of goodness, love and holiness. Remain there for a moment. As you give and receive Sacred Love, healing begins, leading to wellness of body, mind, soul and spirit. Receive the care and protection that flows from the Holy Spirit of God. You are resting in the loving care of God. This is a heavenly place of inner peace. Good and pleasant expectation causes a calm and peaceful feeling. Let yourself move into the stillness of this sensation. Accept Divine Guidance and the unconditional love of God for healing of the Heart.

Breathe in slowly and breathe out slowly, as you become more serene with each breath, and move into a deep state of rest. Do that for a moment, and when you are ready you will continue on your journey into the mind. Imagine within your mind a view in the distance of a flowing stream of blue green bubbling water flowing over glistening rocks of various colors and shapes. There is a clear blue sky. As you rest there begin to review events that have a pleasant loving and helpful influence this present moment.

Now imagine moving toward this mental vision. Become aware of important supportive images. Visualize and understand the learning purpose of any event and then decide what is important for you to accept and what you wish to change. With love and forgiveness, clear your mind of thought and let yourself continue to receive Holy guidance from God's Holy Spirit. Understand that God has the ability to solve any problem. With the help of God's Holy Spirit, begin to work out solutions automatically according to God's perfect will. Take a moment to do that by resting your mind in silence. The Holy Spirit of God is healing your heart, mind and soul. You are a very important, good, person. Sense the surrounding beauty and understand that you are reborn by the power of God's infinite love and caring.

Breathe in slowly and deeply and exhale slowly and deeply. You are peaceful and comfortable. You are secure in the warmth of loving arms. Sense the peace of connecting with God who truly cares. A warm and soothing feeling fills your being. You are one in closeness and loving interaction. You feel completely rested and peaceful. Your mind is free of all care and concern, as you drift into a very pleasant, tranquil state of consciousness. Rest in the silence and when you are ready return with this Holy Sacred Love in your Heart and Soul that is available to extend to all in need. This is Spiritual Healing care of the Heart.

5. Supportive Spiritual Care

To care is more important than to know. Spiritual care requires true concern and compassion for another. Even if a health care giver is a genius and knows everything about medicine, they must still truly care about you in order to be helpful. Someone with less knowledge who truly cares with unconditional love provides a healing presence by the grace of God. This includes the desire and motivation to find answers to problems and needs of the person that they wish to help and heal.

Upon entrance into this life, there is a need for spiritual caring relationships and connection with a nurturing source of support. You are a physical, mental, spiritual being. A relationship in which you give unconditional loving care leads to healing of the whole person. Supportive Spiritual care leads toward present moment living that is important for mental peace. There is a natural need for inner peace and happiness. Fulfillment of this need takes place as you care for yourself and have empathy, compassion and love for others. The soul and spirit requires healing first, and then the physical follows.

The Spiritual caregiver attempts to see life situations as seen by another in order to understand their needs. The purpose is to think with instead of about an individual in order to give spiritual care. "I will become, in a sense, another self for you, an alter ego of your own attitudes and feelings, a safe opportunity for you to discern yourself more clearly, to experience yourself more truly and deeply, in order to choose more significantly." (Carl Rogers)

It is important is to be sincere and honest. All interaction must be genuine. We create and maintain a mutual bond that leads to spiritual growth. Spiritual care requires awareness and concern for the feelings of another person. Recognize and deal with feelings appropriately. You feel with each other but continue to maintain independent control. A mirror image is created in a supportive spiritual relationship. You see yourself in the eyes of another. This is a loving relationship where we touch souls in a bond of faithfulness. True empathy and understanding are a gift of God's Holy Spirit. It is God's way to relate to another person. It is the beginning of enlightenment and elevation to a heightened level of consciousness as you become aware of your connection in the Holy Spirit of Divine loving kindness.

Spiritual Care involves developing a relationship in which genuine concern and caring is a primary focus. It is the ability to convey a true message of understanding for the feelings of another. Genuine feeling is necessary in order for its acceptance as real. The person receiving this holy love feels the warmth and satisfaction of a truly Holy experience.

It is the basis of any therapeutic contact and communication. A requirement for healing is concern and loving interaction. The most powerful healing remedies are faith, hope and love. You have the ability to give love as you begin to truly love and care about yourself. There is understanding of what someone else needs when you know and understand what you need. Nurture and care for your own wellbeing and then let that love extend to include others by the grace of God. The return that you receive exceeds your greatest expectation.

The Reception of Spiritual Care

Dear Lord God, touch my soul with love as I pray and always. Guide, protect and let the light of your love fill my heart. Touch me with the creative energy of your Holy Spirit and the ability to give and receive spiritual loving care. Help me to understand my needs and the feelings of others. Teach me to be caring, loving and compassionate and to be understanding of those who care for me. Thank you God for all your Blessings

Imagine yourself in a magnificent forest. There are towering trees alongside a path in the forest. The dawn of a new day is cool but comfortable. The sun is beginning to rise. The dew on the leaves of the trees is beginning to sparkle as the rising sun extends a glow of light. In the distance are mountains that reveal only a twinkling view of the rising sun. The trees are multiple colors of red, yellow, orange and some remain green. The falling leaves are creating a wonderland of infinite perfection.

You feel very peaceful as you gaze at the falling leaves. The reflection of light through the trees creates an appearance of crystals sparkling throughout the forest. As you walk along the path, become aware of the intricate beauty of nature and the perfection in all things. Every phase of life is so complex and detailed. The perfection and beauty reaches far beyond the human imagination but you have the ability to wonder and become part of that eternal vision of all things.

Now begin to approach a lake. The water is moving in glimmering ripples as the fall wind blows through the trees. You notice that the lake water is shining like a mirror that is reflecting the trees and the multicolored mountains in the distance. A stream of white flowing water is flowing down the mountain. Everything is perfect and beautiful.

You are beginning to feel tired but you know that you are only a short distance from your home where you can rest. The stream leading from the lake continues to flow and create the harmony of the forest. It is peaceful and restful as you inhale the fresh cool clean air. Take a deep breath and feel the sense of total serenity. There is a gentle breeze and the trees give an effect of shimmering and glowing. A rainbow mist is hovering over the lake and a glow of the rising sun is streaming through the clouds.

Home is only a short distance away as you return from an early morning walk. It looks so comfortable and restful. You feel tired and would like to rest. As you walk toward the house to the front door, you feel content to be home where you can rest in a warm and comfortable place. Enter your home now and close the door. There are large windows so you can continue to enjoy the beauty of nature and the falling leaves. There is a fireplace, where you start a fire, watch as it begins to burn, and create glowing warmth. A comfortable reclining chair is there for you to sit and rest. Watch the fire as it burns down; the coals are glowing and radiating warmth and comfort.

As you continue to gaze at the mountains with the falling leaves drifting by your window, your eyes close and you fall into a restful sleep. You are safe and secure, completely protected and comfortable. The heavenly Light of God surrounds you. You know and understand your need for peace, beauty and comfort. You have all that you require and are peaceful and satisfied with yourself and your life. You are a loving, caring person. Love and forgive unconditionally as you love yourself. Understand the feelings of another as you sense your connection and loving bond. Know that you receive the Love of God, now and at all times.

Feel a pleasant sensation of quiet serenity, breathe in deeply and exhale slowly. Each breath is flowing out smoothly and spreading relaxation throughout your body. Listen to the sounds filling the surrounding atmosphere. With each sound, become more peaceful and relaxed. It is now time to rest and replenish your energy. Caring for yourself gives you the ability and energy to care for others.

As you rest in the comfort of your home, become aware of your interactions with others. Feel the connection and blessings that you receive through caring relationships. Only one who cares is helpful and understands the feelings of another. The most important element of spiritual care, is love and belief. You are restoring your entire being to a level of higher consciousness where there is love, kindness and forgiveness. You are self-confident, happy with yourself, kind and considerate. You understand and nurture yourself, this gives you the ability and understanding what you require to care about another. Rest now in the quiet and silence and when you are ready awaken feeling wonderful and rested. Realize your connection with all as you receive this Spiritual Care.

6. Healing Spirit

The Healing Spirit of God is always with us. God is our closest friend and is there when help is needed. Ask and there is an immediate and clear answer. Listen for the voice of God and believe that prayer is answered. God's knowledge, wisdom and intelligence is greater than ours. Therefore, let God, who is much wiser, be our guide and helper. Many people proclaimed healing during prayer and meditation sessions for spiritual care. Personal information is confidential. I think of these healings as God's Work and a very natural occurrence to the point that it becomes a part of hidden memory. There is a tendency to think, this is natural, it just happened, but then there is denial that God is working miracles in our life every day and is always with us.

Healing Love flows from the Holy Spirit of God during meditative prayer. By the Grace of God we are filled with peaceful blessings. Each person is a channel of Sacred Healing Light that is given by the Power of God. Accept this Guidance from the Spirit of God. Have faith, trust and believe that God's Wisdom and knowledge is greater and is caring for all.

God works with those who give care, and the one who receives care. Spiritual Care for health and healing includes prayer, faith and belief, combined with appropriate medical treatment. Healing occurs when we believe and have faith in God's sacred intervention. Meditative Prayer Imagery for Spiritual Care is a method of filling our mind and soul with prayers for faith and healing. What the mind believes the body will follow. Always focus on the power and strength of God's healing light that flows through the Holy Spirit. Visualize yourself as healthy, strong and active. Believe only in the power of God's healing spirit and Love. Always image being in a state of perfect wellness. Believe that God has the power to heal.

Healing restorative energy flows from the Holy Spirit of God. During meditative prayer, this healing spirit reaches our inner being, as we believe, desire and are motivated. There are various methods of spiritual healing. Human interaction is a primary component for healing. The ability to touch the soul and inner being of another through loving spiritual care is a Holy Gift of God.

A gentle touch and loving Care bestows, a God given gift of, inner healing. The human energy field is a perfect parallel image of each person. There is the ability to observe this image as a spiritual body. Thoughts create an immediate reality within the mind. Therefore, always remain focused on the Divine Light of God. As we extend healing prayer with care and love, we nurture the spiritual being of another. During meditative prayer, there is giving and acceptance of the Holy Healing Light of God.

A quiet mind allows the Peace of God to enter the body and soul. Sacred Creative Spiritual power for inner healing fills the body, mind and soul. During prayer there is the ability to explore feelings, and express needs as we receive this sacred healing. Healing prayer requires faith, and a quiet clear mind. During meditative prayer, we move within the channel of the mental and spiritual body. Existence in this form is as clear as in the physical. The soul is reaching a higher level of consciousness.

There is the ability to experience a sense of touch in the spiritual form. We feel without actual physical contact or reach out and touch others and know that all exist in a spiritual environment that has substance. This is a world of thought, a region of consciousness where there is awareness of God's Divine Life Force. The spiritual body flows in a field of Sacred Spirit that is similar to an ocean of gently flowing waves. This is the Spirit of God in which we live.

The human soul is a channel and temple of the Holy Spirit. With God we overcome all obstacles. God's power is working through the person who is directing healing prayer. This ability requires only a desire to support and aid others in need. We then reach an understanding of this blessed experience and use it to help and to heal others and our self. We are living in the Spirit of God and as a gift and by the Grace of God we have the ability to direct this Spiritual creative energy of God for Healing.

Meditative Prayer for Spiritual Healing

Dear God, Thank you for all Your Blessings. Be with me always. Fill my mind and soul with Your Holy Spirit. I pray now for health and wellness of mind, body and soul as it is Your Perfect Will. Fill me with Your Holy Light of healing Love. Help me to focus only on goodness and love. Hold all my loved ones safely in your care. Grant faith and courage to overcome obstacles and let my life be lived in service to You Dear Lord. Fill me with Your Holy Spirit of Light, Guidance and Protection. Grant a Sacred Blessing of Your Spiritual Gift of Healing in order to help and heal all for whom I pray. Thank You God.

Rest in a comfortable position and imagine yourself in a Holy place of peace and sacred healing. Quiet your mind and sense the movement of air around your body. Listen to the sounds of the surrounding atmosphere. Increase your awareness of each sound until you hear with your inner divine mind, which is part of Gods Holy Spirit. See clearer and brighter, until you see with your sacred spiritual eyes. Increase your awareness of all impressions and feelings as you experience them.

Breathe in deeply and exhale slowly as you focus on awareness of your body. Start with your feet and gradually move upward to the top of your head. Feel a gentle vibration of God's Holy Spirit around your head, face, and neck. Let that Holy Light move to encircle your entire body. You are moving into a state of complete peace throughout your entire being. Breathe in deeply and exhale slowly. With each breath, become more peaceful and calm. Understand and listen to the inspiration of Gods Holy Spirit. Rest now and receive inner guidance.

Focus on the sensation of a gently flowing sacred and Holy Light. Create a circle of Holy Light and envision it surrounding your body. This light surrounds and protects you. It is God's Light. It is Loving and Peaceful. You are in touch with God's Divine Source of all power and Love. Your mind is clear and peaceful. Now visualize someone that you wish to pray for. Focus and form a connection in mind and spirit. Always request guidance and assistance from the Holy Spirit of God. Envision God's Holy Light flowing to the one that you are praying for. Become aware of it moving from the Holy Spirit of God as it enters the one for whom you pray. During this state of focused prayer, there is a sense of sacred peace. Clear your mind and quietly wait for guidance.

Let the Holy Light of God move through each particle of the body as needed. As you observe with spiritual vision, there is a vibrant light flowing interchangeably. A feeling of peace and connection becomes evident. Continue moving this flow of God Light for as long as needed and then rest silently and trust that God's Will Be Done. Remain silent in a meditative state as you request further guidance and explore this loving unity, this touch of life.

Learn from this interaction and journey inward. As you meditate, wait for an answer and receive inspiration that is an answer to your prayer. The One and only God for all people is eternal Love and loving. Give and receive this spiritual healing as needed. There is awareness of all life, all beauty and all goodness. When you feel a bond of connection with another, you feel the presence of God's Holy Spirit. Kindness and concern reveals God's Sacred Love with you. Return now, peaceful and calm knowing that you have prayed, cared for another and extended God's healing light and peace.

7. Realization of Wholeness

Realization of wholeness occurs when we learn that Healing is the result of Spiritual Intervention that is a Gift of God. Inner peace leads to Healing of the Whole person. Peace is realized as we quiet our mind and connect with the Holy Light of God within the heart and soul. This means that we are whole and functioning at the highest level of wellness even if a physical illness or injury remains. Medical care is an art rather than a proven science. Usually a percentage of effectiveness is given for most medical treatment. The only true and complete healer is God. We work in and through the Spirit of God. Healing brings together the whole person body, mind, soul and Spirit; it restores the normal state. Health Care Providers are God's helpers, they prepare the way for healing.

The way is prepared through the use of spiritual care that promotes health and healing. It is important to correct the underlying cause of a problem. It is often necessary to change behavior, environment and beliefs. To heal is to make sound or whole and to restore to the highest level of wellness that is possible. Separation from fragments of our own soul and God causes problems. Healing brings together the whole person. It restores the normal state. Healing can take place even in the presence of illness. Healing is restoration to health, but the definition "making whole" is different from curing. You can cure a specific body part or disease, but healing includes the entire being.

We each have personal needs and problems requiring an individual plan based on specific issues. This includes emotional and mental factors. Use effective methods of spiritual self-care. Adapt to each situation by having faith and trust that God is in charge and taking care of us and all whom we love. Focus on the present moment and think good uplifting thoughts. Remain in control of your feelings through right thinking. Become aware of your feelings and take effective action through problem solving and practicing methods of relaxation and mental imagery including meditative prayer.

As we enter a place of peace and silence, there is an increase in perception and ability to receive uplifting spiritual strength for healing. Begin to become more alert, aware and involved in the spiritual power that surrounds and fills our entire being. Increase in awareness of each characteristic of life. During meditative prayer and heighten consciousness, there is a sense of the natural flow of God's spiritual presence. As the Light of God enters our life that which was once a dull image now becomes brighter and clearer. It is similar to receiving sight that was lost. This leads to spiritual holy insight and inner healing.

The presence of God's Holy Healing Light is perceived during meditative prayer. Sacred bonding within the Spirit of God occurs. All Healing begins with God, who is the foundation and creator of life. God's life force transcends beyond all known cosmic planes. The power that we feel and observe in all objects is the result of connection with this Sanctified Creative Spirit, extending strength for inner healing. A Spiritual reality exists outside the realm of physical experience. It is attainable by inner reflection rather than through knowledge based on sense impressions. We have the ability to image this perception of life beyond the realm of physical experience. Inner vision and wisdom are a gift of God's Holy Spirit. Through the faculty of sacred inspiration, all senses are in harmony with the Holy Spirit of God. We then become God's channel of healing, guidance and love.

The One and only God for all people is endless and extending into all eternity, love and loving. God is boundless and yet special and individual as a friend. This is all life, all beauty and all love. You clarify reality through meditative prayer for spiritual care and healing. This occurs naturally in a caring relationship. Empathy and compassion initiate God's flow of Healing Light which creates a sense of interactive healing energy that flows freely for peace and inner healing. Spiritual healing is an experience that leads to a mutual exchange of healing light that is helpful to each person. Divine Love is close to you at all times. When love transcends the boundaries of ordinary existence into an atmosphere of beauty, the result is spiritual bonding and new life.

It is the Spirit of God's Love that motivates us to help and care about others in a manner that is spiritual and yet personal and natural. Simply caring about another, leads to an elevation in consciousness and realization of our wholeness. Empathy and understanding are a natural part of a sacred spiritual relationship. Meditative Prayer and loving spiritual care leads to healing of the whole person. Each person has the ability to reach this level of mystical awareness. As we focus our mind in a state of meditation, divine awareness of Holy Light Energy for inner healing becomes a reality. You are then prepared as God's channel of spiritual healing. This is a realization of wholeness and awareness that we are one and living in the Spirit of God.

Spiritual Wholeness

Dear God, Help me to find a place of peace, clarity, receptiveness and Divine Guidance as I pray and meditate. Lead me to a place of inner vision where Sanctified Healing Light flows freely to help and to heal, as it is Your Perfect Will. Make me a channel of Divine Peace, Love and Healing. Be with me always to guide and protect. Fill my mind heart and soul with the Holy Spirit of Love.

With each inspiration, imagine your breath flowing out and causing a sense of relaxation throughout your body. So, feel that relaxation. Take a deep breath now. Breathe in slowly, and feel a sense of peace entering your mind, body and soul; breathe out and become aware of an atmosphere of serenity. Take another deep breath and exhale slowly. Continue to feel more at ease now, calm and content. Your mind is becoming receptive to Holy Guidance. This will cause a deep and lasting impression within your mind that will remain for as long as required, in a perfect way just for you. You are moving into a deep peaceful state of relaxation.

Rest now and allow yourself to enjoy this very peaceful, relaxed state of being. Your conscious mind can rest completely. Your inner mind will receive and understand all that you receive. Now imagine yourself in a very peaceful and beautiful place. There are tall trees and flowering plants. The colors are bright and give an appearance of glowing as the sun shines over the clear waters of a running stream. White fluffy clouds are moving slowly across the horizon. The air feels so clean and fresh. It is so beautiful and pleasant that you automatically move into a deep state of inner peace.

The sun is glistening on the stream and the moving waters splash against the stones forming white bubbling pools of water. As desired, lean forward and look into the water. Rest there for a moment and receive guidance and awareness of love that is unconditional. A sense of peace and contentment fills your mind and soul. Now become aware of a flow of the Light of God healing your life. You are in tune with God's Holy Spirit as you rest in quiet meditation. This is a form of spiritual growth that leads to wholeness.

Request guidance from God and Sense yourself in the presence of Sacred Holy Light. Mentally ask God for Holy inspiration and guidance for extending healing Light. Receive guidance from the divine mind of God. Within your mind, experience yourself in the Presence of God. With your eyes closed, look up within your mind and envision a pure white light rising up through your body and bonding in a Spirit of Holiness. Request guidance and accept this state of grace.

Only Divine goodness has any influence. God's light surrounds and protects you. Feel the light moving through your body and to your hands. Envision the light flowing toward one or many for whom you pray. Let this light flow according to Holy inspiration, and then give thanks for this guidance. Receive this Divine Light for Spiritual wholeness and healing. As you give to others, you also, receive healing love. Return with complete confidence and faith that you accomplished your intension in God's perfect way during this meditative prayer. Return with the ability to remain in God's Holy Presence. With this knowledge, you are peaceful and confident. You are feeling good both mentally and physically and begin a new way of living in a heavenly place of peace and healing for spiritual wholeness.

8. The Compassionate Way

"The Lord, God, compassionate and gracious, slow to anger, and abounding in loving kindness and truth." (Exodus 34:6) (1)

The compassionate way is God's way. Spiritual care, given with loving kindness and true concern, is a compassionate way of living that brings peace. Inspiration for compassionate interaction and loving spiritual care flows from the mind and heart of God. This must be genuine for it to be helpful. We intuitively know when someone truly cares. It is reflected in one's eyes, speech and manner of interaction. God's way is a real way of experiencing the sacred peace of a healing relationship. When this type of compassionate bonding occurs, it is a gift of God.

Preparation of the mind and soul are prerequisites to the experience of compassionate spiritual care. Meditative prayer is a method of conditioning the mind to become clear and peaceful. A pure mind is devoted to others and aware of the intricate function of all living things. Love and appreciation of the nature of another requires seeing the other as an extension of our self. At times it may be necessary to have actually felt what the other is feeling in order to identify with their feelings. Otherwise the use of imagination is helpful. Think of what it is like to be in the position of another. We put our self in their place for the moment and realize what is needed in order to truly be of help in the care of this child and creation of God. When we know what we would want, there is some understanding of the needs of each person. We must also realize that each is an individual with personal needs and that good communication is required. Ask and gather any and all information that is available. Good care also requires planning according to the individual problems.

All are one in the living Body of God. All bond in a loving relationship. Quiet meditation inspires compassion and understanding. Each act or thought given with loving kindness has an immediate effect that is shared with all in a bond of compassionate spiritual care. The Holy Spirit of God inspires empathy and compassion for others. As we pray and meditate we then teach others to do the same. Learning to relax the mind and body leads to healing. This is the way to spiritual understanding and emotional peace. Compassion that inspires constructive action is the principle foundation for inner healing, harmony and peace. We are divinely inspired and of one mind in a spirit of caring and loving kindness. Devotion to others creates inspiration for living in the Spirit of God where only good exits. A kind and loving attitude advances into an expression of affection that is a blessing to all. Giving of self-promotes spiritual Growth.

Our purpose is to develop empathetic, compassionate relationships. Compassion and caring becomes a natural response as we work to create a true and genuine feeling of loving concern that leads to Heaven on Earth. This is home where all unite in spirit. It is a great mission to care. Developing a sense of compassion, leads to a vision of perfection within the mind that grows into a physical reality. This inspiration for compassionate living in the Spirit of God reveals the promise of Living on Earth as it is in Heaven.

Feeling of Compassion

Dear God, be with me as I pray and meditate. Be my helper and guide and help me to know your will in my life. Let only your goodness and love guide my way. Help me to listen and understand so that I will truly be a blessing to others and receive Divine grace and peace in my life. I thank You, Amen

Rest in a place where you are comfortable. Imagine gentle ripples moving along a stream of clear water. Focus your attention on the moving water. Rest your eyes and within your mind imagine a gentle sensation of peace. Feel a wave of relaxation flowing gently through your body. Now as you rest there, relax all the muscles of your face for a moment. Let your scalp relax... your forehead... eyelids... and your cheeks. ... Especially relax the muscles around your mouth and lips. Just allow all the muscles in your face let go. Now relax your neck. ... Let your shoulders relax. ... Feel your neck and shoulders relaxing completely. ... Eliminate any tension that may be in any of these areas. ... Let that sense of relaxation move throughout your entire body.

Rest now, by quieting your thoughts and entering that silent place of peacefulness within your mind. Transfer your awareness from the outer reality to a place of peace within your mind. Imagine yourself protected and cared for. You are safe and secure in the Spirit of God. This is a place of understanding and compassion for all. You are a part of and one with all of life. You are living in the light of God. Rest, as you begin to understand the importance of this concept.

Breathe in deeply and exhale slowly. Sense the Holy Spirit of God surrounding and filling your entire being. This is warm, soothing and yet sacred and awe-inspiring. You feel as though you are embraced in the arms of a very kind and loving friend as you become aware of the Love of God. With each breath, rest your mind and body, as you become more aware of a sense of compassion. Let your thoughts just flow by, as on a moving stream of peaceful water.

Focus or imagine a moment in time in which you receive kindness, consideration and concern. Become aware of this feeling. Giving is as rewarding and blessed as receiving. As you give to others, you receive equally. Compassion is the creation of a mutual bond of caring and concern. It elevates your mind and soul to a higher level of consciousness. You are a spiritual being. You are kind, loving, and compassionate. You have the ability to place yourself within the spiritual realm of another in order to help and promote healing. You are a channel of love, a channel of healing, a channel of guidance and enlightenment. You are God's helper as you understand your spiritual nature and grow in your ability to care and have compassion for all.

As you extend loving kindness, goodness and love, you are doing God's work. You are aware of your bond and connection with all of creation and have the ability to place yourself within the spiritual realm of another in order to help and promote healing. You are a channel of love and extend healing, guidance and enlightenment. These are the qualities of a compassionate and caring individual. Return now and become aware, of the air that you breathe, the surrounding sounds, and the sensation of your body. You are feeling rested and refreshed as you sense the Love of God within your heart.

9. The Nature of a Loving God

"You shall love the Lord your God with all your heart, and with all your soul, and with all your strength, and with all your mind; and your neighbor as yourself." (Luke 10:27) (1)

During Meditative prayer our focus is the Love of God and bonding in Love. How do I love you Dear God? I Love all that you are. I love only good and all that is good. I love all of Your Glorious Creation, all people, loved ones and family. I love peace, happiness, compassion and only goodness. I love the perfection in all things, the good and the beauty. I love harmony and order. I ask for guidance to see, hear, and feel only according to your will. I give to You Dear God, myself, to be one with Your Holy Spirit, as a loving child and friend. Teach me your way and make it my way. I thank you Dear Lord. Love of one of God's children is love for God.

Love is a feeling that flows naturally but an act of Love is controlled by the free will. Even if we don't feel love there is the ability to act with love. This is a blessed and selfless act of Love. If we perform a loving deed only for the Love of God, we are doing God's work. This type of love is given freely. The only reward is knowing that of our own free will, there is acceptance and desire to live according to the Will of God. Those who Love are living in the Spirit of God and God lives in them.

It is the Nature of a Loving God is to heal emotional pain and discomfort. Mental pain can be at times worse than physical illness. Emotion or feeling and learning to cope with life circumstances related to feeling is of major importance in the spiritual care of yourself and others. Our mind and thoughts, to an extent, influence and even control feelings. Therefore the ability to quiet our thoughts and rest our mind is necessary for care related to emotional issues. It is a fact that feelings are triggered by thought and can be changed according to thought. Thought not only influences feelings, there is also an immediate effect on bodily function and the status of one's health.

There are feelings however that appear to be completely separate from mental control or thought. Love often appears without purpose or reason. Suddenly there is Love. This includes love for any person even when there is no possibility of the love being returned. It is a chemical reaction, without thought and just appears and sometime disappears as abruptly as it materialized. The one who is loved is the most important reason for living. The loved one is only good, perfect and adored in the mind of the lover. This type of love does have a Divine and Holy purpose. It is a blessing and spiritual lesson in what love is and how we are to interact with those whom we love.

It is our spiritual purpose and mission to Love One Another Unconditionally. Unconditional love is the unrestricted giving and acceptance of kindness, caring and compassion. It is the ability to feel with and create a loving bond in order to become part of the life of another as we blend with all life. We nurture and create this state of mind within our self. Certain feelings of love seem to appear naturally and automatically. Unconditional love begins in the mind as you recall the love that exists between you the creator and all creation since the beginning. God is Love and the source of all Love. We then decide to give spiritual love unconditionally. The recollection of that Love, even when the actual feeling has faded away, always remains and teaches the mind and soul how to give the sacred love of God.

Fulfillment of this need takes place as we enter a caring relationship. A connection in which we give unconditional love inevitably leads to a spiritual communion with God. This spiritual and loving care leads toward wholeness. There is a natural desire for acceptance and love. As we give love, we receive love. This becomes clear as we help others and give support and aid to those in need. Love creates a channel of healing. Spiritual care generates creative energy as we become aware that God's love is unconditional. We then develop a spiritual bond that is of heavenly origin. This connection is a divine bonding in a caring relationship.

Unconditional love is a spiritual gift given by God. We learn to love, when our mind is focused on God's heavenly realm of Holy Love, during meditative prayer. Love requires only the desire to love without expectation of return or compensation. The recipient of that love has only to accept this gift. The expression of unconditional love reveals that this love is special because it is then our decision to give this gift that we receive from the divine without expectation of return. The Love of God is as the flow of a current in an ocean stream. It is compelling, as a natural force, acting mutually and causing a pure and perfect union. This generates a field of Holy spiritual energy that is directed in a specific flow for healing.

When love is unconditional, each is boundless because all that one accomplishes is a mirror image of the other. View the image of your reflection in the stream of consciousness and view the image of your love. As you feel this love in your heart, it will enlighten your entire being. We then truly sense the restorative touch of God's Love and enter a healing relationship. This is Spiritual Care that flows from the Spirit of God. "Beloved, let us love one another, for love is from God; and everyone who loves is born of God and knows God. The one who does not love does not know God, for God is love." (1 John 4.8) (1)

Emotional Healing of the Heart

Imagine now that you are standing in a picturesque and peaceful garden. It is a pleasant warm day. The fragrance of lovely flowers enriches your feeling of quietness. As you walk through the garden, experience the beauty of divinely colored flowers. Notice a quaint staircase; walk toward the stairs and begin to walk up. With each step, move closer into a heavenly light and divine presence. Birds are chirping in the trees and there is a soothing breeze.

There is a sense of inner peace and calmness as you walk up each step. You are very comfortable and feel the calmness of this peaceful environment. Experience this sensation of peace and contentment. You feel pleasant, and rested. As you walk up the stairs and reach the upper level of this magnificent garden; there is a brook of clear moving water. Look into this clear water and notice the sun shining on the surface of the water. The rays of the sun exhibit an aura of rainbow hues in the mist. Sense the impression of total silence as though time was suddenly still. Remain, for the moment, in the present. Just be there, and accept Holy guidance from the Spirit of God.

You are feeling a pleasant sensation of quiet serenity, breathe in deeply and exhale slowly. Each breath is flowing out smoothly, and spreading relaxation throughout your body. Listen to the sounds filling the surrounding atmosphere. With each sound, become more peaceful and relaxed. Your inner mind is always aware, as you rest in God's Divine Presence. There is a flow of the Unconditional Love of God. Feel the caress of God's loving presence. This is a touch of God's Love. This is the Love of God for humanity manifesting in a bond of spiritual Loving Care. All is existing in the Sacred Presence of the Creator who is All Love and Loving. In this state of awareness, all remains stable. You are One or as two parts of one being.

To give Unconditional Love is a Sacred Act of God. It is a Spiritual Transformation of your mind and Soul. You move to a greater level of Blessed Understanding. There is perception, not only your own feelings, but also empathy for others. This leads to peace in that by the Grace of God, you are directing your own life. You are living in the present moment with God. This is a powerful restorative healing factor. Experience this life giving living water, as you live in the Holy Presence of God. When love is unconditional, you know yourself personally, as part of your Love, and as part God and all creation. God is Love.

As you care for yourself, you care for others. Love always creates. Love is only good and creates only happiness for all involved. Two become of one of mind, heart and soul. The Spiritual energy associated with a caring relationship is loving and peaceful. As you become aware of this sense of togetherness there is trust in God; only good can exist where love is real. As you return, walking slowly down the steps, bring this sacred consciousness with you and live in the Spirit of God's Holy Love and Sacred Blessings.

10. Our Angel Guardians

"An angel is a pure spirit created by God. The Old Testament theology included the belief in angels; the name applied to certain spiritual beings or intelligences of heavenly residence, employed by God as the ministers of His will." "Although the word "angel" in the Bible, meaning a messenger, nearly always applies to heavenly beings, it can occasionally apply to human messengers."(catholic.org/saints/angels/) Angels are one with and an extension of God. There is a place within your heart where we find God's Angels. All are one with God in this place of Holiness.

Meditative Prayer is a way to awareness of our Angelic helpers of God who guide and protect us. An Angelic encounter is a blessed and sacred experience that is given by the Grace of God. The purpose of an Angelic presence is as a messenger and helper of God. They are Heavenly Beings who are filled with the Spirit of God and bring help, and God's healing during times of need. During Meditative Prayer, there is increased awareness of this sacred gift of Divine Spirit. We are accepting of the Goodness that is God's Reality. Faith and belief in the perfection of God's

Holy Will initiates miracles. We create and act as an angelic channel of God's Love to extend healing, peace, guidance, and protection.

There are numerous accounts of angelic intervention. A few years ago, while riding in a car as a passenger, I started to fall asleep and was warned in a dream like state by a messenger of God, who appeared as a little child, to stay awake and watch the driver. Within a short time I noticed that the car was going off the road and was headed down a ditch toward a wall. It seemed as though time suddenly slowed down. I had time to notice what was happening. I awaken the sleeping driver in time for him to abruptly turn toward the road. There was damage as the car scraped the side of the wall but no injuries to anyone. A car moving at approximately 70 mph should have hit the wall instantly; but, there was a warning and a miraculous slowing of time. This was the work of angels.

A clear and serene mind generates Holy Inspiration for healing, guidance and angelic assistance in any situation. Our mind receives and accepts inspired information for many different purposes. The conscious mind discerns and directs thoughts that are received from God who is Only Good. Healing occurs as we accept health-giving Holy Inspiration for the mind, body, and soul. There is a Divine Purpose on this Earth, as in Heaven. Kindness and loving care is the substance that builds a healing environment. Its purpose is to heal the mind and soul. Spiritual care with love promotes peace and healing. We are working with God's Angels when we help others.

The experience of changing adversity into miracles is a wondrous healing experience and an objective worth pursuing. During meditative prayer our inner mind is aware of only peace and joy in the present moment. Faith and trust that God is caring, kind and loving lead to a place of precise and total healing. Each detail of life is observed in exact and in perfect order.

All people are a creation of love and beauty formed in the image of the Creator. There is consciousness of self as a perfect child of God. We are touched by Sacred Angelic Light when, through prayer and meditation, guidance for understanding God's plan becomes part of our life. We are a sacred design joined with God's Holy Spirit. We are blessed by God with the presence of Angelic Guardians who are guiding us toward Living in the Spirit of God.

Touched by Angelic Light

Rest now and pray. Envision yourself entering a sacred place where you are peaceful and secure in the presence of Angel Guardians. This is a place for revitalization of mind, body, and soul. Close your eyes and within your mind envision the atmosphere filling with a beautiful mist of white light. This light fills the surrounding area. It is peaceful and soothing to your mind body and soul. Clear your mind and begin to sense this healing Angelic Light throughout your body.

You are protected and secure in God's Holy Light. There is a sensation of loving kindness and a feeling of healing light filling your entire being. The intricate design of your being becomes clear, as you image within your mind this Angelic healing. It is creating intricate patterns of restorative power. Become aware of God's Love as it supplies your soul with Angelic Light for inner healing and guidance.

Continue to be aware of this atmosphere of serenity; your entire being is healing as it is God's Will. The Spirit of God performs the mission of renewal. You are refreshed and vibrant in this design for living in the Spirit of God. A feeling of peacefulness and security is apparent. You receive unconditional love and care by the Grace of God. Joy is complete and eternal as you are touched by Angelic Light for Inner Healing.

Your mind now again begins to focus on the Holy Light. The flow and movement is tender and comforting. Complete confidence in the purpose of this experience is certain. You are living in the Spirit of God. This is a place of contentment and sacred peace that leads to inner healing. You view all life with clarity. A sense of fulfillment is apparent as the sensation of satisfaction and loving care becomes visible.

Inner healing of your entire life begins. You are healing in mind, body and soul. Your entire being is renewed and healed in a perfect way just for you. Sense the touch of Angelic Light and you are living in the Spirit of God; an atmosphere of love and peace. You are now waking in the light of this beautiful day. You have received the spirit of God for inner healing. This is healing of mind, body, and soul. Know that love is always there for you and present with you now and forever as you return to the present moment. You are touched by Angelic Light of Inner Healing.

11. Sacred Awareness

Counsel, the third gift of the Holy Spirit, is the fulfillment of the essential virtue of prudence or judgment. Prudence is a practice used by many but counsel is mystical. We are able to judge how to act properly almost by intuition or foresight. Because of the gift of counsel, we have the courage to proclaim the truth of the Faith, because the Holy Spirit will guide us in defending those truths.

Counsel is a form of Sacred Awareness. We have the ability to understand through sacred Holy insight. We are blessed with the ability to view life completely including the subtle factors that are usually unseen. All things become clear as inner sight is increased. This clarifies our vision of God's reality which is only good. Living in the Spirit of God is a manifestation of Sacred Awareness. Human beings are a creation, inspired by the sense of feeling and love. Communicate with God in meditative prayer and focus only on the goodness that flows from God's reality. Sacred awareness increases our ability to appreciate God's Creation. Awareness of a sacred relationship at a higher level of consciousness clarifies the spiritual senses.

Awareness begins with the sense of feeling and perception. Interpretation of feeling is individual. Each person perceives things differently. The sense of vision and hearing combined with thought help to determine individual perception of reality. Thoughts are a very powerful force which cause an immediate physical and emotional reaction. What we think and believe determines our perception of reality. Think as God thinks. Sacred awareness is having the ability to perceive reality as it is God's will. See as God sees, hear as God hears and accept only that which is good and of God. There is a Divine Plan for all of existence.

We think and feel as one and function in harmony with all existing life. The components of life are eternal, expanding and changing in its form of perception. During prayer and meditation we receive inspiration that leads to mental peace. Holy inspiration is a design for living that is formed and shaped into beliefs and perception of life. This inspiration flows from the Holy Spirit of God. We see beauty and perfection in all of God's creation.

Sacred Awareness is the ability to view with the spiritual senses. An important function of meditative prayer is to bring this Holy inspiration into the process of living. This is a function of seeing with intuitive inner vision which is a gift of God's Holy Spirit. During meditative prayer there is a spiritual bonding within the mind of God. We enter the world of Divine reality which clarifies perception of the outer world. There is the ability to see and feel people places and objects in a true and perfect light. It is where acceptance and loving concern transforms emotions of into vital spirit for peaceful and joyful living. Sacred Awareness and harmonious union of mind, body, and spirit is God's purpose.

The ability to receive inspiration that leads to understanding a situation is needed for healing and developing trust that God is only good. It is important to be aware of what we perceive. Consciously increase sensitivity to the beauty in all things. Reach out from within the mind and find the truth. This is our own private world that is just between us and God. The inner mind is composed of intricate and complex systems. All of existence is a permanent record in Divine memory. A pattern of all that we see, hear and experience exists within the Spirit of God.

All knowledge is contained within the Divine mind. Sacred Awareness brings this knowledge and insight into the light where it can be used for guidance and healing. Mental systems contain all soul memory including life patterns and genetic heritage. As we journey into the inner mind, we clarify our inner vision of reality and transform, through the Spirit of God, all into enlightenment and peace. Become aware of all life and see God's true light.

Develop a Sense of Sacred Awareness

Rest now in a comfortable position, close your eyes and pray. Ask God to help, guide and fill you with the Holy Spirit. Just imagine yourself walking along an ocean path on a beautiful summer day. It is the dawn of a new day and there is a slight flicker of the rising sun ahead of you. You feel a warm soothing breeze that is refreshing. Listen to the sound of the ocean waves and begin to feel very peaceful and calm. As you view the ocean, notice small boats floating on the calm sea. The rising sun is beginning to reflect on the moving water and is creating an aura of harmony as the waves sparkle like moving particles of orange light. You are developing your natural ability to be alert, attentive and aware of the beauty and intricacy of all things.

Feel the warmth of the rising sun flowing throughout your entire being. Just focus on the sensation of peace and light for a moment. Continue to become more aware of the beauty and peace. As you rest on a nearby bench, position yourself facing the ocean. Become more comfortable as the reflecting Light spreads throughout your body. The glistening light of this beautiful day fills you with a sensation of total contentment and peace as God's inner healing begins. Rest there for a moment.

You are a magnificent creation of God, conceived in love and born to be a feeling, compassionate person. You are always cared for and the Holy Spirit is always with you. So begin now to feel that sense of love that emanates from within. Begin by focusing on your physical sensations. Close your eyes and become aware of the sensation of your eyelids touching each other. Notice any sensation around your eyes and let them rest.

Focus on any visual image that may appear and make it as real and specific as you can imagine. Listen attentively to the sounds that vibrate from within and the sounds of your outer surroundings. Consciously become aware of any sensations. Always be aware of what your body is telling you through Holy inspiration. Experience your inner feelings with a sense of sacred peace. Only goodness that extends from the Spirit of God is influencing your emotions and behavior. Sacred Awareness is the key to healing and happiness. God is the healer of all. Spiritual Healing is becoming aware and mindful of feelings and needs, you then trust that you are loved and cared for. Then begin to implement a healing remedy. You are living in the Spirit of God who is providing that healing in a perfect way just for you.

Only Holy and sacred goodness can influence you in any way. You are always in control. You are peaceful and calm. A sense of contentment and joy is becoming evident. The sacred light of God surrounds you. Clear your mind now and rest there in silence as inner healing occurs. Let the feeling of love remain with you. God's Love fills your being to maintain balance and wellness in your life. Understand that you create your feelings by your thought. Sacred awareness leads to mindfulness of the Holy Spirit of God in your life. You have the ability to see, experience and feel with clear and perfect sacred awareness. You are the director of your life; through God's gift of free will.

12. Bridge of Heavenly Light

"We have come to know and have believed the love which God has for us. God is love, and the one who abides in love abides in God, and God abides in him. By this, love is perfected with us, so that we may have confidence in the Day of Judgment; because as He is, so also are we in this world." (1 John 4:15-17) (1)

Meditative Prayer is a bridge to God. We learn to peacefully move over the bridge to Live in the Spirit of God. *"God is Love, and the one who abides in Love abides in God, and God abides in him."* (1) The feeling of love is a form of Heavenly Inspiration that occurs naturally. It is a gift and a blessing from God. Genuine Love generates power for healing and joy. It is always a channel of good because it is God. As we focus on loving and kind thought, we experience the reality of this inspiration. Love acts as a bridge within the mind that leads to a sacred reality. Within the human mind, there is a way that leads to God's divine mind. Through meditative prayer, there is the ability to dream, visualize, feel and extend inner vision into an experience that is a true expression of Divine and Holy Love Abiding in us.

The feeling inspired by Love creates a sensation of flight above the ordinary that is a healing of the mind, body and soul. It provides energy and power that gives new life. Eventually it is necessary to return to stable ground. At times it may lead to the necessity to swim or sink. But Love always remains a gift and miracle that inspires a caring heart. The feeling of Love may fade but the memory and knowledge of Love is eternal because God is Love. That memory leads to a compassionate and understanding person.

Spiritual Care given with Love provides great power for inner healing. It is a bridge of heavenly light that remains within our heart forever. We are together forever in the Light of Love. Feelings create awareness and power. Loving and kind feelings lead to a heavenly peaceful existence within the mind and soul. This creates a special place of Sacred Love that is always there for us because it flows from a place of Divine Holiness. Within the Love and Peace of God, there is advancement toward a field of awareness that leads to freedom.

The power of Love that is of God can change your inner awareness and the outer world. Love is much more than a feeling. Within our mind, there is a Sacred Source of Love, inner peace and healing. Thought causes feeling, and we become aware of Love through feeling. There is always the ability to act with loving kindness. This is our Human God Given Gift of freedom. An act of Love generates a chain reaction that leads to a Bridge of Heavenly God Light.

During meditative prayer, envision the good in all by seeing a beloved friend in all people. Give Love and know that we possess the right of passage over the Bridge of God's Heavenly Light. Love initiates inner peace and healing as we enter that place of sanctified silence in the Loving Embrace of God. Our mind is a Bridge to God for inner healing. This is a place of Devotion where we are always welcome. Now we have the ability to journey to this place, just relax and receive inner guidance as we focus only on kind and loving sensation, God will lead the way to Heavenly Light. We are living in the Spirit of God who is Love.

Finding God's Heavenly Light

Begin with prayer. Imagine yourself embraced by the loving arms of God. Ask for guidance and the Holy Presence of Love. Breathe in deeply and exhale slowly. Imagine the air vibrating with particles of light that extend a sensation of inner peace and Loving Care. With each breath, become more rested and calm. Imagine yourself crossing over a bridge to a place of beauty and peace. In this place you are one with the Holy Light of God. Envision yourself, surrounded and filled with God's Holy and Healing Light. You are moving through a mist of glistening white light. It is soothing and peaceful. Everything is bright and clear. Just become aware of the silence as you glide closer to this Sacred and Heavenly Light. It is so enchanting to sense the brilliant surroundings as you rest and become aware of a Blessed atmosphere.

Continue to become more peaceful; breathe slowly and feel the freshness of the air. Your contentment increases, as you clear your mind now and just listen and wait for guidance. Only good, inspiration, or feeling can influence you in any way. Blessed Spiritual Love fills and surrounds you. You are embraced by the Light and Love of God. Love creates this special place.

Continue to breathe in deeply and exhale slowly. You are entering a state of complete relaxation. This is a place of rest and peace. It is exactly where you want to be. Contentment is a place within your mind but you will find it anywhere in the physical reality by clearing your mind for the moment and enter that silent place with God. Just be there for a moment. It is all that you need. Remain there, in the silence. A sense of total relaxation of your mind and body is becoming evident. You are one in spirit, one in love, now and forever.

You may return to this place at any time. Do this with reverence and a pure loving heart. It is your connection with the Love of God. During meditative prayer, God heals your soul and your body. Have faith and trust in the healing power of God. In your physical existence, finding Transcendent Love is a seemingly slow process. Within the dimensions of God's heavenly kingdom all is possible. As you enter a level of consciousness beyond the physical, all is accomplished according to the perfect will of God. The Bridge of Heavenly Light is found through the Love of your Life.

13. Spiritual Care of the Soul

"He restores my soul; He guides me in the paths of righteousness For His name's sake." Psalm 23:3) (1) Spiritual Care of the Soul is caring for that part of the person that in many religious and philosophical beliefs, is the spiritual and immortal essence of a living being. There are multiple definitions of the soul. It is part of ancient beliefs and history since our know beginning and mentioned approximately three hundred times in the Bible. All living creatures possess a soul that is eternal but the Human Soul was given a gift of free will. This gift of free will gave us the knowledge of good and evil. The animals and all of God's creation are free of the knowledge of adversity. They are good, sinless and united with God. All that occurs is a normal and natural circle of life. God is Love and there is absence of fear, trust and sacred peace.

The gift of free will gave the Human Soul the ability to know right from wrong. There is only perfect and divine order that is set into exact motion from the beginning. Our Human Nature gave the ability to act in a manner that is contrary to Divine Order. Mankind is the only being that has the ability to upset the balance of nature. Spiritual Care of the soul is a way of returning to the perfect Love and Order of God. We learned to fear and separated from the Love of God when we lost sight of the fact that Love is the only true reality and that God is Love.

"There is no fear in love; but perfect love casts out fear. (1 John 4: 18) (1) Spiritual Care of the Soul creates a peaceful and loving heart. Love is often the cause of worry, anxiety and serious concern for those whom we love. To Love is to Care. It is difficult to eliminate these emotions but it is important to understand that this is the result of our own fear and lack of trust that God is in charge of each situation. Perfect Love, leads to a peaceful mind as we become aware of God's truth. Fear is a form of darkness that is dissipated in the Love Light of the Creator. Adversity causes disruption and darkness within the soul, the Light of Love eliminates darkness. There is a flow of Holy Inspiration and inner peace as we focus, in meditative prayer, on the goodness of God's creation.

Spiritual Care of the soul includes developing Holy Vision and insight into God's perfect way. Observe the kingdom of created form and life. Know that only an intelligent mind is the creator of such perfection. The organization of universal knowledge is God's Sacred Power. Spiritual care of the Soul requires God's gift of Holy Insight that becomes miraculously clear as we focus on peaceful, loving thoughts. Become aware of the perfection and beauty in all things. Look closely, and use all physical senses, to observe the intricacies and beauty of creation.

Spiritual care of the soul helps us to gain insight into God's Reality which is only good and perfect. There is love for all people and all of creation. Meditative prayer transforms our mind and soul; it leads to a place of learning life's mission and purpose. Clarity of purpose and awareness of the true self is important for spiritual care. This becomes clear as we meditate and enter a sacred place with God. From each of our physical senses there is a flow of God's Holy Spirit. Prayer, to extend God's Love, leads to Spiritual growth. We are in tune with a higher level of sacred and Holy Awareness that flows from God's Holy Spirit. This leads to peace and Spiritual Loving Care of the Soul.

There is comfort and enlightenment as we begin to know our self personally and as part of all. As we move into God's reality, we experience the presence of abiding Love. Our soul is elevated to a level of Holy and sacred awareness. A flow of God's Holy Spirit touches our life. The Human Spirit is a miraculous being, we have the ability to accomplish great things. As we accept God's Love, it flows like a wave of spiritual power that evolves into a physical and spiritual expression. Love of God is Love of our Brother, Sister and Love for All. This is Spiritual Care of the Soul in the Holy Presence of God.

Spiritual Care of the Soul for Holy Presence

Pray and rest in a comfortable position; you are filled and protected by God's Holy Light. Imagine a ripple of peaceful, calming and Holy, Spiritual energy moving throughout your mind and body. This is the Spirit of God, the Light of God. Sense it moving throughout your body. You are becoming peaceful and calm now, and have a clear understand of where this journey is leading you. Take a moment for silent prayer. Understand that you accept only guidance that flows from God who the source of infinite good.

With each breath, continue to become more serene and content. Now breathe in, exhaling slowly, feeling calm, at ease, flowing, at peace. You can continue now breathing easily and becoming more peaceful. Your mind is clear and receptive. It is like a river receiving replenishment from a flowing stream, ready to encounter sacred peace and to see clearly. You are at ease feeling good. Continue to relax more peacefully. Breathe easily and deeply. You are becoming more composed, joyful and at ease with each breath. Feel a wave of relaxation flowing gently as the ripples of a peaceful stream of flowing water. The Holy Light of God surrounds and protects you at all times. Only good and the power of God's light and love can influence you in any way. You are secure, calm and peaceful.

Rest now, by entering that silent place within your mind. From this place, you will reach out from within your mind to connect with God's Holy Spirit. Just be there as though you are waiting for a door to open and allow you to enter. This is the doorway to inner peace within the Spirit of God. It is a path leading toward inner vision. Belief and faith, in this awakening to the Sacred Light, is a major elevation in consciousness.

Continue this focus with a clear mind. As thoughts begin to enter your mind, allow them to pass. Just be there. Remain quiet and peaceful becoming more relaxed as that flow of Holy Light clears your spiritual vision. View peacefully this window of timeless existence and move deeper into a more calm and composed state of mind. Now, the light begins to flow like a stream of water, glistening and flowing into your mind, clearing the way to your destination. It becomes brighter until it emanates from your entire being forming a reflecting aura of sacred Light. As this light surrounds your body, you are protected and secure.

You are now ready to reach for Divine guidance. See the door opening, feel the peace and listen to the sounds. Objects and places become clear as crystal water. Just rest in the silence and wait for guidance. You open a gate to the infinite and sacred mind leading to God. Your inner sight becomes amazingly clear. With the power of this inner vision, view from within and become aware of God's guidance and assistance. Thank God for the blessings you have received. Become alert and aware of the sacred perfection in all of life and God's Holy Presence.

14. Living in the Spirit of God's Forgiveness

"So do not fear, for I am with you; do not be dismayed, for I am your God. I will strengthen you and help you; I will uphold you with my righteous right hand. (1) (Isaiah 41: 10)

Only goodness exists when you are living in the Spirit of God's Forgiveness. God loves us and forgives all transgression even when our beliefs are opposing God's Divine natural law. This Earth is a place of dreams and illusion. In many circumstances, we rationalize that specific behavior is necessary and appropriate. The human mind is aware of serious adversity, but the adversity is transformed into something that appears acceptable. Difficulty is seen as a part of life that is tolerated because it appears as unchangeable. In order to change the world, we must use our God given freedom and ability to change our own mind.

God is only good. God's plan includes Divine justice which is part of the natural scheme of existence. Every action causes a reaction that occurs naturally according to the scheme of Divine creation. If we put our hand into fire it will be burned. But, where is the true reality? I attended a fire walking class in which the participants walked on burning coals and remained completely free of injury. Now we see dimly but as we awaken to the Light of God, we will see clearly. Beginning with one person at a time, we allow only good to enter the mind, heart and soul and act accordingly. This is the power of God's forgiving Love that is unconditional and without exception. Only the Love of God is real. Through trust and faith, there is seen only, the light of knowing, that all things and all people are safely cared for in the Hands of God.

Goodness and light are the true reality. Realize that forgiveness is an essential component for finding peace and happiness. Forgiveness is a bridge to the inner experience of feeling for another unconditionally. It leads to peaceful living in the Spirit of God. This is the nature of forgiveness in a caring relationship. You are living in the Holy Spirit of God, as you love and forgive. Happiness and peace is unlimited. The true meaning of life leads to inner healing and living in the Holy Spirit of God. This means that, one person at a time, we learn to love each other. There is a beautiful song that begins with "Let there be peace on Earth and let it begin with me." (Jill Jackson Miller and Sy Miller)

Forgiveness for Living in the Spirit of God

Always begin with prayer and as you pray, with each inspiration, imagine the light of God filling your entire being and causing a sense of quiet peace throughout your body. So feel that relaxation. Take a deep breath now and breathe out slowly feeling any tension leaving your body. Take another deep breath and exhale slowly feeling more and more at ease now, calm and content. You are moving into a very peaceful state of relaxation. Drift and dream now feeling calm and in control as you allow yourself to enjoy this pleasant, relaxed state of being. Your conscious mind can rest completely. Your inner mind will receive and understand all that the Spirt of God reveals. Ask God for forgiveness and forgive all in return.

Forgiveness leads to eternal life in God's Holy Spirit of Love. The way is prepared by God, leading you, to a place of forgiveness, where all unite as one. In this place, the stillness fills and touches the atmosphere with a feeling of limitless goodness and Love.

Abide in Love the Sacred Presence of God

Just imagine yourself resting comfortably in a Heavenly Place. Heaven is anything and everything that you want it to be. You are blessed by God with the ability to freely choose. Image your perfect reality. Create an image of Heaven within your mind. Feel secure in knowing that you have the free will to change this image at any time. Of your own free will, live according to God's Will. There is only goodness in this Holy Place. God's Kingdom is eternal and existing here, now in the presence of this moment.

There is a great need for closeness so move your right hand out toward the right and open it. Now, Move your left hand out to the left and open it. Request that God's Holy Light of Love and clear vision flow through your hands at the center of your palms. Sense the Light of God moving through your opened palms and throughout your body. Now let your hands move slowly toward each other. As your hands meet, let your palms touch each other with your palms pointed upward. Let one thumb cross over the other as your hands join. These are praying hands moved together from right to left and joined as one. As we become one we are loving and Living in the Spirit of God. God's name is the name that you have given to God. This is given with Love so great that you are willing to give all to bring us into that place of Spiritual Oneness. Dear God, I thank you for this inspiration.

Visualize and image yourself in a sacred restful environment. You are blessed by the Holy Spirit of God who is the foundation of all loving kindness. Your purpose is just to rest there knowing and understanding the peace and contentment a forgiving heart. During this visit to a place of living in the Spirit of God, you know that all are one in love. There is knowledge and a sense of eternally belonging. Love for one includes concern and caring for all. A loving heart cares and forgives. This restful state of consciousness is a path that is leading you to living in the spirit of God. You find all that you need or want. As you receive guidance, the path becomes clear and healing occurs. Images evolve into reality and inner healing takes place.

Clear your mind and rest the in silence. There is freedom to receive the benefits of a loving relationship. Within this state of consciousness, you are in touch with the Spirit of God that lives within you. Forgiving and caring about another is an act of selflessness leading to unlimited awareness, connection and unity. The self then grows, but as one with all and living in the Spirit of God's forgiveness.

15. Spiritual Care of the Heart

The human heart is a sacred center of feelings and emotion; it is the symbol of love. A clear mind and a loving heart act as a gateway to a state of sacred devotion to God. Spiritual care of the heart consists of learning to live in a place of inner peace and love. Emotional states have an important effect on our health. Loving, kind, and peaceful thoughts and feelings are healers of the soul. Thoughts influence feelings and bodily processes that control our ability to enter a loving relationship. A calm state of mind improves our sense of peace and our ability to live in a place of spiritual Love and goodness.

Connection with the Light of God is the only true source of inner peace. The power of our mind and intelligent thought, that is a Divine gift, can assist us to gain control of feelings and our life. The mind is the creator of feelings. God is the creator of goodness. When feelings are causing sadness or unhappiness pray for guidance and trust that God is caring for you. Believe that with the help of God we will find inner peace. A peaceful mind is the gateway to wisdom and understanding of each situation. During prayer we find a means of solving problems through Divine guidance. Ask for guidance from God in all situations. Then attune thoughts with God's Spirit of peace and holiness. As we receive guidance, we live in the Spirit of God and Abide in Love where all is well and peaceful. This is possible through faith and trust that God is always there to assist and guide.

It is important to increase our awareness of feelings in order to discover the cause. Being aware of feelings, helps us find a solution. Pray and talk to God, express personal feelings and needs. Ask that only God's perfect will be done. It is always God's will that we are well, happy and peaceful. God knows the way to help in any situation. Realize, recognize and deal with feelings in a manner that leads to inner peace and healing through the Spirit Love.

An emotion causes a response including certain physical, mental and spiritual changes. There is a faster or slower heart rate, decreased or increased functioning of certain glands, and changes in body temperature. In many instances, we are not consciously aware regarding the reason for a feeling. There may be a vague awareness of a situation without knowledge of a reason. It is natural to avoid unpleasant emotion. Therefore, it is important to learn methods of peaceful relaxation, imagery and prayer. Live in the present moment with God. Place all in the hands of God. Preparation of our mind to do this is vital. Prepare through focus on only that which is good. Learn the art of meditative prayer in order to clear the mind for receiving Holy Inspiration and love that flows from the Heart of the Creator. Know that God Loves Us.

Feelings that are inspired by the Love of God lead to Sacred Peace. Loving thought, action, and feelings become meaningful messages to the internal environment of our soul and lead to a place of Holy Love. Focusing our thought on the peace of God is a way of healing that is important for mind, body and soul. Events in life leave lasting impressions that influence our ability to quiet thoughts and find a place of inner peace and Love with God. The reason for a sensation or feeling may be unavailable to the conscious mind. It is then necessary to trust, have faith and let God heal us. Focus only on thoughts of love, peace and healing that promote happiness and contentment. Live within the Holy Spirit of God and know that only the Love of God has any influence in life.

As we journey into the silence of the soul seek only the Holy Spirit of God. Avoid outward thought. Think only good and focus on the Love of God. Thought is the creator of feeling and reality related to feeling. Feeling begins with a thought but becomes an actual experience as it is accepted. Begin by clearing the mind and remain in the present moment. Pray and focus on thoughts of the Goodness of God. Believe that we will find God's Holy and perfect way. Remain in the present moment. We have free will that is a gift of God and we are in control of our life and feelings. Good feeling are a healing remedy for our heart and soul that lead us to the Spirit of God.

Care of the Heart and Soul

Rest in a comfortable position, pray, and ask that God's Holy Spirit be with you. Relax all your muscles from the top of our head to the bottom of your feet. Begin to feel a movement or vibration throughout your body as you rest. Within your mind imagine a circle of light around yourself and sense a flow of gentle energy encircling your body. As this flow of God's Holy spiritual energy continues, become more peaceful and relaxed. A soothing vibration conveys a sense of connection with all of God's Creation. Now as the light, flows remain focused. Become aware of the feeling of serenity. As you rest, realize and understand God wants you to be happy and to feel good. You are loved and cared for at all times.

Now, you are going to participate in a healing experience. Image within your mind a clear vision, of a place, of Heavenly beauty and peace. Take a deep breath and exhale slowly. Take another deep breath and exhale slowly. Become aware of breathing in, and out. Experience the feeling of breathing. With each breath feel the pure vital life energy entering your lungs. Relax now, and breathe normally and naturally.

You are resting in the presence of this moment where all is peaceful, relaxing and soothing each part of your body. Focus your attention on the top of your head. Look up with your eyes closed through the top of your head and visualize a pure beautiful light. Imagine this light being unlimited, as it enters your body. Begin to drift now into a deep state of peaceful relaxation. As the light surrounds you, there is knowledge of protection, peace, and healing.

Thoughts directly or indirectly lead to feelings. You are learning to develop your ability to remain focused on the present moment with God and to avoid all thought during meditative prayer. Your physical senses identify the way you understand yourself, and your interpretation of life situations. You are now becoming aware that you have the ability to access inner beliefs that cause feelings. You are in control of your thoughts and your life. It is your decision to focus only on pleasant, kind, loving feelings that lead to peace and happiness. Love is a feeling that involves your total being. Its power extends toward the infinite. Once you have cleared your mind, remain in the peace of the sacred silence.

Let the Holy Spirit of God be your guide. Only good flows from the Spirit of God. Listen closely only to the word of God. Resting in the Silence leads to serenity. Truth, love and peace flow from the mind of God. Rest within the Peace of this sacred present moment. Feel the love within your heart and soul as you live in the Spirit of God.

16. Knowledge of Self

"Then the Lord God said, "Behold, the man has become like one of Us, knowing good and evil; and now, he might stretch out his hand, and take also from the tree of life, and eat, and live forever"(Genesis 3:5) (1)

"To know yourself is to know God." This is an ancient principle quoted by many spiritual masters. The Human Soul is a temple of God's Holy Spirit. You are a timeless being who is a child of God. The Self who is one with God, is found within, this is why Jesus Christ said: "The Kingdom of Heaven is within you." "Blessed are the poor in spirit, for theirs is the kingdom of heaven." (Matthew 13:24) (1) As we extend the Self through spiritual growth, the human soul connects with the Light. The Christ Light is the Light of the God that illuminates heaven on this earth leading to truth and knowledge of self.

Awareness is to be gradually focused within during meditative prayer. One must know the Self in order to know God. Meditation is a profound spiritual practice. The way to self-awareness includes self-observation. God guides and enlightens us to know our selves; this fulfills the reason of life. The most mystical, and divine occurrence is to unconditionally know one's Self.

It is not selfish but selfless to know the Self bonded in Divine Unity with the Creator. It is the most reflective and deep gift in life. Life is divinely planned to lead us to this peak of knowing the Self. It may be a distant journey through the maze of conscious living. But, if we hold out our hand toward Holy guidance, the light will appear. The soul meets with God, in oneness, peace and eternal Love. This is a sacred endeavor. Vital creative energy, intelligence and infinite memory form our soul pattern. Awareness of the true self brings awareness of our spiritual self in oneness with the creator. We then become a complete channel of kindness, love, caring and compassion.

A sense of awareness of self becomes evident through inner guidance from the Light of God during meditation. We are revitalized in an environment of peace. There is an awakening in the Light of God. This sense of sacred togetherness expands to the point of recognition of the genuine self. It is the fulfillment of our life mission because all that is needed becomes part of our self-concept. Now the reality of each moment is apparent. We are living on Earth as it is in Heaven. Our relationship with all of God's creation is now in the Light.

Knowledge of your Spiritual Self

Begin with prayer and rest in a comfortable position. Clear your mind and search your heart and soul. Understand that you are a good, kind and caring person. You have the ability to reach the highest levels of awareness. This will lead you to comprehension that is far beyond the ordinary. You are one and part of all things. You are an individual and yet connected in Spirit with God, the essence of all existence. Realization of the vastness of your inner being creates an image of infinite beauty and perfection. As you increase in self-awareness, a vision of beauty and perfection in the nature of all things becomes evident. Within yourself, is connection with God Who is the source of all goodness. There is an unending sea of spirit that expands beyond imagination.

Begin now to increase your awareness of this vision of reality as you meditate and imagine within your mind. Focus your attention on relaxing each part of your body. Imagine yourself resting in a very special place of peace and comfort. You are surrounded and protected by the Holy Light of God. Feel yourself moving forward and upward toward this silent place of beauty and light. In this place, you are completely secure and protected by the Holy Spirit, as you begin to feel and accept a pure and Divine Healing light entering your mind and body. Your inner awareness is increasing as you rest.

You are aware of reaching the deepest levels of your mind. Your inner vision and understanding is increasing. You are reaching higher levels of consciousness and perception. As you move toward that still silent place within your mind, begin to feel more relaxed, pleasant and peaceful. Experience yourself drifting into a state of perfect stillness, perfect love and perfect connection with God. Just let go and be at peace. Feel yourself moving in the direction of the greatest levels of soul recognition.

You are entering that stillness of mind, where all are one. Become aware of the sensation of inner peace. Your mind is still, clear of thought and ready to receive Holy guidance from the Spirit of God. Be still and feel the sense of peacefulness. Become aware of your breathing. Feel the movement of each breath. Become conscious of the air that you breathe. Breathe in, deepening each inhalation, and exhale slowly. Breathe in and out, as you experience total relaxation. Your purpose is to increase your understanding, become more conscious, knowing, feeling and self-aware.

Experience your body sensations. Observe every perception no matter how light or subtle. Feel the sensations that you are experiencing. Feel the Life in each part of your body. It is calm, pleasurable and soothing. Timelessness is an experience related to ordinary things, the gentle touch of the hand, a smile, the sounds of nature and the movement of the air through the trees. Just quiet your mind and become aware of the sensations of your body. Perceive this Holy and sacred power at work and feel the nearness of the Creator within. Remain aware of this presence with you always.

Clear your mind of thought and listen quietly. The Holy Spirit of God is your Guide and protector. There is a view in the distance of white soft clouds. Continue to become more peaceful and calm by viewing these clouds within your mind as they take form and slowly change. As you do this, trust that the divine order of the creator is in total control. Prayer is power in the world of the sacred. Experience yourself according to the Holy Will of God who is only good. Pray that only God's perfect will be done now and always.

Ask God to allow your mind to review any incident that may be influencing, your life in the present. When the scene appears, you may alter or change it according to the guidance of God's Holy Spirit Who is with you always. Believe and have faith that God is the builder of your life. Trust that only good will influence you in any way. Let your mind remain clear until a picture appears. You are peaceful and calm. You can see and feel in a clear mature manner. Let the Holy Spirit be your Guide. Feel loved and nurtured. Feel loving care, peaceful and understand the meaning, and need for this peace. Understand that all occurrences are a learning process leading to a favorable purpose.

Knowledge of yourself in unity with God and all creation is clearly visible in the Light of God. Just remain there in complete peace and silence for the moment and when you are ready return. The Holy Light of God is protecting, guiding and enlightening your life.

17. Consciousness of the Spirit

Spiritual Care includes is the art of caring for the entire person including body, mind, soul. Healing is a process of integration or bringing together into harmony all aspects of the individual. Incorporating the spiritual nature into a plan of care is necessary for providing complete care of the whole person. Each person has individual beliefs and ways of expressing their spirituality. Behavior, status of health and emotions are often a direct result of spiritual motivation. Many people are not religious but everyone is in some way spiritual. Knowledge of the nature of our spirituality is an important part of care. Spiritual beliefs needs, and problems are assessed and considered when planning care.

Meditative Prayer is a method of increasing consciousness of our spiritual nature. We remain in the present moment and pray for guidance and enlightenment from the Holy Spirit of God. Imagery then helps us to explore inner feelings and increase awareness of our spiritual being. This peaceful state of mind helps to increase our understanding of the Holy

Wisdom of God. Guidance through Holy Inner Vision leads to healing.

Connection with God and bonding in the Holy Spirit generates the ability to function creatively. It joins the lost parts of the soul in order to become emotionally complete. The body is matter, meaning that is has weight and takes up space. The Spirit is the universal energy and power of the Creator that causes the individual to have life. The mind, with ability to think is also spirit or non-physical. It is the regulator of intelligence, emotion, and feelings. The soul is who we are as an individual. Mind, spirit and God's Gift of free will compose the Human Soul.

Free will gives us our individuality. We know that we have free will because there is the human ability to function separately from will of God. Without free will, there would be just the Sacred Goodness of God; but, that would also eliminate individual spirit or soul. All forms of nature function only by instinct and the power of God. God's creatures are a perfect and exquisite extension of Divine Spirit. Animals are sinless because they are unaware of the existence of sin. Their soul is universal and connected in the spirit of God. All animals exist in the realm of Heaven or the Spirit of God eternally. Mankind acquired the knowledge of good and evil through disobedience. Adam and Eve ate of the forbidden fruit and lost connection with God. The way to return to God is to bond in spirit; of our own free will, to surrender to the will of God. This causes the self to grow into oneness with God, and continue to maintain individuality, as intended at the time of Divine Creation.

Consciousness of the Spirit of God within and part of our being is to be recognized in order to live in the Spirit of God as a true friend of God. We are living in a physical body, powered by the Holy Spirit and controlled by our mind and intelligence. Individual free will is the consciousness of the self as a person who is separate from others. It is our purpose to understand our needs and to learn to fulfill our desire according the will of God. Become aware of feelings and understand our connection with others in a way that is good for all. This requires knowledge of the genuine self who is one with God.

The self or the ego is the caretaker, keeping watch, between who we are as an individual and a vast universal consciousness. Our purpose is ego growth and communion within the Spirit of God. The ego grows but is simultaneously diminished into the oneness of God. The sense of self, however, remains with knowledge of self and yet one with the Creator. Without self-esteem and love we cease to exist and the ego disintegrates. We must know how to love our self in order to understand how to love another. Love God and love your neighbor as you love yourself. (1)

It is necessary to create a balance between self and the mind of God. We are to flow with God and grow but always maintain awareness of who we are as an individual. Our purpose is to live according to God's Will by using our own free will. We are to join with God Willingly. Otherwise it would have no purpose. God created mankind to be a friend not a puppet on a string. We are created to pull our own strings. The individuality grows to merge with God as one surrenders to God's Holy Will. This requires Consciousness of the Spirit.

There is a difference between being selfish or egotistical and ego growth. As we grow, we know our self but are in harmony with that universal consciousness of God. In a sense, our personal ego has expanded beyond the limits of self-consciousness but is now in the realm of cosmic consciousness. This is a universal ultimate purpose. Self must grow to become one with all. Then there is knowledge of how to love self and others. Our purpose is spiritual growth and clarity. Connection and bonding in spirit with God produces the courage, trust and faith. There is a Sacred Connection with all and yet, individuality remains. This is the design of human creation.

There is Consciousness of Spirit and Oneness with Humanity. The lost parts of our being are retrieved. The Human Soul gives mankind a separate and personal identity. Independent decision, is a primary human characteristic that no other species possesses. Human free, will with the help of God, unites the segments of our personality into a complete whole. God's will is done, using your own free will.

The will or soul gives humanity a special higher form of existence because there is the ability to function independently. Humanity is to become conscious of self, and to bond with God in all of creation. Incorporate the knowledge of self into the whole without losing individuality. The individual mind is then working harmoniously within the Holy Spirit God.

During meditative prayer, explore innermost feelings leading to clear understanding and inner vision. Visualize and become aware of the eternal goodness and sacredness of the Creator. Our mission is to transform the soul and increase Consciousness of the Spirit of Holiness within us. All are one within the Holy and Sacred stream of consciousness. Just as the sea, creatures live in the ocean. The natural component of our being merges with the spiritual and divine quality of life. This is consciousness of Spirit which is a touch of life and an awakening and movement into the Holy Light of God.

A Spiritual Dimension of Consciousness

Always begin with prayer as you rest in a comfortable position, and breathe in deeply. As you exhale, begin to become aware of a sensation of absolute peace. God's Holy Spirit is with you always to protect and guide you. There is a place within your mind in which you are aware of a spiritual dimension of consciousness. You have the ability to enter this place. It is just between awakening and sleep. With the help of God, you are in complete control of all that occurs within your mind. Now you will rest your mind and body, as you become aware of God's Holy Presence during meditative prayer.

Clear your mind of all thought for a moment. You are entering a pleasant place of sacred awareness. Become mindful that all is good, perfect and beautiful. You are secure as you sense a flow of Divine strength. There is a sense of complete safety. Your mind is resting in the present moment. Become attuned to the infinite beauty of living. You exist within an atmosphere of exquisite perfection. This is God's Holy Spirit of creative energy. Living in the Holy Spirit of God's Love sustains sacred spiritual communion and inner peace. You are increasing in your consciousness of the Spiritual Realm of the Creator.

Your spiritual self is energetic, alive, creative and fulfilled. This is your true nature. You are a whole person who is bonded with the Holy Spirit of God. This connection leaves your inner self peaceful, calm and in control. It is a cause of peace and contentment. This is where life-giving needs are satisfied. You are conscious of yourself and of your connection with the creator. This is a mystical communion within the being of the Creator.

Abide in Love the Sacred Presence of God

Love is part of your being. You are united with the source of all life. All that is necessary is the knowledge and recognition of this gift. Nurturing your inner being through prayer and contemplation leads to freedom of the soul to live in the Holy Spirit of Love. Become aware of a true image of yourself. You know that there is the ability to experience genuine freedom as you grow in the Spirit of Holiness.

Let a gentle flow of relaxation surround and fill your body, as you move into a very peaceful state of rest. Imagine now, see and feel yourself, walking in a beautiful forest. Notice in the distance a clearing. Walk to this location. There is a small log cabin. You are invited to enter by a very kind and caring friend. It is beautifully furnished and equipped with all that you need. You are secure and protected. You are free from any disturbance and rest in a comfortable chair. Just be there for a moment. This is a journey to a special place within your mind. You find anything desired in this place. You have the ability to create within your mind a perfect place of comfort and peace just for you. Only good, will influence you in any way. Only good is of God. Allow only a pleasant and peaceful experience. Remain there in silence, and wait for guidance.

A sensation of stillness and order fills the surrounding atmosphere. It is so comforting and restful. You can view through a large window a stream of clear water flowing through a beautiful valley. The mountains in the distance are bright and clear as the sun casts a glow upon the moving waters. As you focus your attention on the gleaming water, move into a peaceful state of relaxation.

Become aware now of God's Holy Spirit filling you with a sense of peace and harmony. Silence your mind of all thought. Let inner guidance that flows from God's Holy Spirit transform and soothe your mind and soul. Take a few moments to remain in silence. Your mind is now clear and free to receive Holy Inspiration. A sense of peace and contentment fills your mind and soul. Now there is awareness, and spiritual consciousness of God's Holy Presence with you at all times. In this Holy Place thought is reality. You have the ability to communicate with all who you know and love. You have entered a Spiritual Dimension of Consciousness in the Holy Spirit of God

18. Raise up Your Soul

"Give Thanks to the Risen Lord"

"Yet those who wait for the LORD Will gain new strength; They will mount up with wings like eagles, They will run and not get tired, They will walk and not become weary"(Isaiah 40:31) (1)

The above photograph was taken on Easter Sunday at Sunrise Service 2015, as we sang the words "Give Thanks to the Risen Lord". Many would consider this a coincidence, I think of it as a sign from God that we also are created with the destiny to rise up our human soul and become aware of God's Holy Light in Our Life.

"According to the spiritual principle of human beings, the soul is the subject of human consciousness and freedom; soul and body together form one unique human nature. Each human soul is individual and immortal, immediately created by God. The soul does not die with the body, from which it is separated by death, and with which it will be reunited in the final resurrection."(2)

The soul is defined as the spiritual part of the individual. The Human being is created in the image of God and is animated by the Spirit of God. The body and soul work together in harmony according to a Divine plan. The Human Body filled with the spirit of God is a temple of sanctified holiness. God has created it and will raise it up. "The unity of soul and body is so profound that one has to consider the soul to be the "form" of the body. It is because of its spiritual soul that the body, made of matter, becomes a living, human body; spirit and matter, in man, are not two natures united, but rather their union forms a single nature.

The Church teaches that every soul is created by God and that it is immortal. It does not perish when it separates from the body at death."(2) The Church teaches that spirit is distinct from the soul. Spirit implies that from creation man is structured to a mystical completion and that the soul through grace will be raised beyond that which it merits to communion with God. The spiritual tradition of the Church also emphasizes the heart, in the biblical wisdom, is where the person decides for or against God. (2)

Our Human Soul is seeking the way, in its journey toward communion with God. The human self has disconnected with the spiritual self. Now we are searching for the way back, the way home to God. The soul is in pursuit of renewal and reawakening to our spiritual nature and connection with God. Recovery of the soul leads to Sacred God Consciousness. The ego or the self is the keeper of the door to Holy consciousness. It is our decision and free will, given by God, to accept only the will of God. Through meditative prayer we receive and accept guidance and inspiration from a Sacred and Higher source of consciousness that is only good. Our purpose is to bring this knowledge and understanding into the physical reality. There is then reunion of the whole person in the Spirit of God.

During Meditative Prayer, the inner mind has the ability to review images of events in our life that have a significant influence on health and wellbeing. It is important to explore the nature of these impressions. We all have feelings, but if they are due to an internal response to external conditions such as mental injury, it is necessary to stop, rest our mind and body and determine the nature of the situation. When an individual is defeated often enough and long enough, there is a retreat. The soul is overwhelmed and there is an attempt to delude this world. The soul, then overcome with individual problems, loses trust in its connection with the spiritual nature and connection with God. Lack of faith and trust in the power of God to care for all our needs results in spiritual darkness.

The mind affects the delicate balance of the body. This has an effect on the physical, emotional and mental health. It is necessary to regain trust in God and attend to problems in a way that leads to health and healing. Mental pain can be more devastating than physical illness. Pain signifies the division of the wholeness of the human being. We have fallen into darkness and pray that God will raise us up into the Holy Light. With the help of God, we have the power to create contentment and peace in our life. This power and ability exists within our self, who is connected to the Holy Spirit of God. Begin now to change adversity leading to health and healing of body, mind, and soul. The basic purpose of meditative prayer is spiritual growth leading to a higher level of awareness, health, and freedom from discomfort. God will raise us up to an increased level of spiritual awareness, insight and inner vision that leads to understanding. Meditative prayer and imagery now inspires us toward a raising up, and home, to God.

Homecoming of the Soul

Rest now, in a comfortable location. Pray and ask God to guide and protect you. Close your eyes, and relax as you begin to create pleasant images within your mind. Imagine yourself resting in a very beautiful and perfect place just for you. This is a special quiet place where you are peaceful, happy and protected. Only good and pleasant thoughts or feelings will influence you in any way. This is a place within your mind. It is a place of spiritual substance. You are always in total control as you remain focused only on the goodness of God. Create a sacred place of peace and beauty within your mind by using distinct mental prayer and imaging. God's Holy Spirit is leading you toward a heightened level of spiritual awareness where you are home with God and living in the Holy Spirit.

As you rest, imagine yourself viewing a circle of Holy God Light directly in front of you. Imagine this sacred light slowly moving forward, and then upward. As it, moves follow it within your mind. Mentally, move forward toward the light. As you continue, feel yourself floating upward. Become aware and realize that you have the ability to be free in divine spirit. Your mind and soul are free to explore all the wonders of infinite creation. Just be there for a moment, feeling peaceful and calm. Enjoy the serenity and accept inner guidance from God. Your spiritual awareness is increasing.

Within your mind pray and ask God to lead you closer to His Holy and Healing Light. Experience and feel the Light of God embracing you with Sacred and Holy Love which leaves you uplifted and peaceful due to the complement to your soul. You enter this life as a beautiful and perfect child of God. This image of perfection will always remain. Become aware of that perfect inner child and understand that this is who you are. You are born into an atmosphere of divine love that is always with you and part of you.

Mentally clarify any life event, in a perfect way, through the Holy Spiritual guidance that flows from God. This is leading to spiritual growth, healing and renewal of your soul. The power of God in you leads to a higher level of consciousness. An ideal image of your self leads you closer to home with God. You create in your life that which you image and believe through faith and trust in God.

Focus on the good and eliminate thought of adversity. The Holy Spirit of God is always with you. You are loved and cared for. You are a good, kind and caring person. A deep connection exists between all people. The true reality is in the present moment which is the only place to create this Holy and sacred mental outlook. See clearly with the sacred gift of spiritual vision. You are a child of God who is loved. You are home and living in the Spirit of God.

19. The Spiritual Self

During a vivid dream like meditative state, I was in a large room with a mirror at the end of a hall. I walked to the mirror wearing a long white dress with a veil covering my head and hair. Only my face is visible. This is all that you are; do not think much of the things of the world in this life. Love is Selfless, but the evolved Self is an individual who is part of all Love. (3)

It is difficult to avoid thinking of the things of this world that interfere with our peace and happiness. We care and therefore we are concerned about the problems and needs of those whom we love and of all people. How do we avoid worry, anxiety and fear not especially for our self but for all who we love? We are as one in this life and the problems of one person has an effect on many.

Think only of that which is of Heaven. Give to God all who are loved and trust in God's ability to care for them. Trust in God eliminates worry.

Detach with everlasting and total unconditional Love. Help others, but know the limitations of humanity. It is only with faith and trust in God that peace is found. Recall the dream vision. This is all that we are as Human beings. Think only of the things of God, who is caring for all of His children and our children, on this Earth as it is in heaven. Let go with complete and total love in heart, mind and soul.

Belief systems are formed throughout life. As we accept ideas and transmit them to our inner mind, they become part of our individual creed and part of our character. During meditative prayer, guidance leads to transformation for nurturing and healing the inner self. Clear perception of a situation is increased and we are guided by God.

The genuine self is the person that God created us to be. It is our ideal and we have the ability to connect with this image of perfection. Each person is a perfect child of God, as we believe, this image becomes part of our life. Allow only thoughts of that which we know to be consistent with our perfected self-image. This is the true self-image. This is our Spiritual Self.

Awareness of your Spiritual Self

Dear God, I pray to separate from the things of this World and move closer to you Lord God. I move now to a place of heavenly accord. Forgive me for any fear, worry or anxiety because they lead me away from You Lord God. Fill me now with Your Spirit of Peace. I thank you for all things of this earth and in Heaven. Take a deep breath, and breathe in Love and Peace. Breathe out any adversity and live in God's Light, in the Spirit of God's World. This is Heaven on Earth. I pray that all find peace through you dear Lord God in this world which is Your World.

You are God's Child and God cares about you. "I want you to be happy and peaceful, for as you are I Am." Thank you dear Lord God. Help me now to clear my mind of all adversity and fill my mind with only thought of your goodness and peace. I surrender all who I know and Love into your care and believe that all is well now with my heart, soul, and mind.

Recall yourself as that beautiful baby and child. Find an image of beauty within you and know that this is you. It is who you really are, waiting to emerge like a growing flower, that is the immortal being hidden behind a veil waiting to be revealed. It is now time to let your inner Spiritual self, free to accomplish all your God given intensions. Think only of the things of God in this world; remember and recall its spiritual nature, inner beauty and infinite perfection.

As you gain access to God's Holy place of Light and Peace, become aware that your evolved self is a Spiritual being who is part of God and all love and goodness. Your genuine self is peaceful and content. This is your true nature. You are receiving guidance that will direct and give knowledge that is leading to inner peace. Your focus is on awareness and learning methods of dealing with events that lead to inner wellbeing through trust and faith in the power of God to care for all. This will increase your understanding that brings peace and healing.

Rest in a quiet place where you will be free of disturbance. Image within your mind your special place where you are peaceful and secure. Mentally be there and with each breath, become more relaxed and calm. Pray and know that you are guided and protected by the Holy Spirit of God. Now focus on a journey within your mind.

See, feel and hear yourself, walking through flawlessly picturesque mountain valleys and over small hills. It is a warm glassy brilliant day. The sound of a flowing stream adds to the splendor of the day. As you gaze toward the horizon, notice the setting sun. It appears as a large red yellow ball. The reflection on the surrounding atmosphere gives the effect of a rainbow sky forming into velvety clusters of slowly moving clouds. You are awed with the beauty of God's divine creation.

You are beginning to feel tired. It has been a long and beautiful day. Sit to rest and continue watching the setting sun as it disappears in the distance. The sky is getting darker but the air remains warm and fresh. There is a gentle cooling breeze. The stars begin to appear, lighting the night sky and twinkling like diamond lights in the heavens.

As you sit there, enjoying the peacefulness of the evening and the heavenly atmosphere, a soothing drowsiness fills your senses. You feel as though your eyes are heavy and closing. The sound of the crickets and small animals is like a lullaby. Notice the sound of soft music and begin to walk along the path to the place where the sound is flowing through the silence of the night.

The music is flowing from a glass dome. As you reach the entrance and go inside, there is a feeling of being completely protected and secure. There is knowledge of protection from any adverse influence or intrusion. A shield of Holy light energy surrounds you. Millions of stars are lighting the sky. The moon is new and glowing with a rainbow aura. The music is playing softly and you feel so comfortable. There are large soft white satin cushions where you may rest and dream pleasantly.

You are experiencing a deep, peaceful sense of contentment as you move into a more comfortable state of relaxation. During this state of relaxation, increase your awareness of all the things in nature functioning in perfect order. As you gaze into the heavens, harmony and perfect universal order, from within and without, becomes an undeniable reality.

Just as all things work in perfect order according to God's plan, your spiritual self is working to resolve any problem. You realize that God is clarifying your understanding of the true reality. Inner Holy guidance from God gives you the ability to arrange all information and understand it from an entirely distinct viewpoint. You may review this information completely and realize that there is the ability to obtain total freedom from any problem.

As you trust and have faith in God belief systems automatically and naturally changes in a perfect manner according to God's Holy will. The effect of this change is becoming more evident each day. As you drift into a more peaceful state of relaxation, your inner mind is guided, by the Holy Spirit of God, to work out solutions that assist you in any situation influencing your life. Your inner mind is aware of your connection with the sacred holiness of the Creator. You are aware of all your feelings, impressions and beliefs. With the help of God you can examine these beliefs through Holy guidance and work out methods of resolving any difficulty. Within your mind, there is always a place of peace with God to resolve obstacles. You transform beliefs into a positive enriching influence.

Continue to rest now. It is the morning of a new day, the sun is rising and a beautiful day has dawned. You feel wonderful in every way. You are rested and refreshed. Outside of the dome are towering mountains and a waterfall. The clear water is flowing into a mountain stream. It is warm and refreshing. You move into the stream and feel a sense of complete purity from within and without.

A soothing healing and Holy Light, the Light of God is flowing effortlessly through your physical, mental and spiritual being. God is clearing any obstacle. Your genuine self is energetic, alive, creative and fulfilled. This is your true nature. Your physical being is an image of your Spiritual self. Awake to the Light of God and feel wonderful in every way, realizing that God is in guiding and protecting of your life, thoughts, and feelings, in harmony with your Spiritual self.

20. Sacred Gateway to Justification

"For one who believes from the heart will be justified" (Romans 10:10).

Recently I had a dream. I walked through a gateway and into a beautiful immense opened space. There was a magnificent large stage and beautiful comfortable seats available for a huge audience. I noticed that my husband and other family members were sitting in the audience. As I entered the area, the audience was to my right and a long table was on my left. I turned toward the table on the left which was covered with various types of exquisite mystical, spiritual items and books that were there to take without charge. There were people dressed in white gowns and others in various brilliant colors of the rainbow. Everything was very real, vivid and detailed. I was amazed at how beautiful everything was but wondering where I was and how I got there. I walked to the end of the table and asked someone about my location and how I got there. I was told that I came through the valley. I accepted this answer very peacefully and without any concern. I was told that everyone was waiting to greet me and again observed the audience and familiar faces. I was guided, in my mind, to walk to the center of the stage and up a few steps on to the stage where I was honored and accepted. I noticed that I was dressed in a beautiful long gown. It was a weave of various colors especially a brilliant green plaid. Rose petals were falling and covered the ground which appeared as white marble. There was a white vivid curtain in front of me as a stage background but I could still see people, walking in the distance and socializing, as though it were transparent. I was told, all that I wanted or needed was here for me. I was guided to kneel in front of the curtain to acknowledge that I reached a place of sacred grace. As an honor, and in recognition of this attainment, a cross with a rose was hung in the center of the curtain. This inspired me to recall memories of spiritual and religious ceremonies; one of which included roses. I then started to think that my daughter would love this and looked toward the doorway to see her enter as I awakened and thanked God for the blessing of a beautiful dream.

There are many ancient and mystical meanings for the Rose and the Cross. They are associated with various mystery organizations and spiritual groups. I was not aware however before the dream that a Lutheran Symbol is the Luther Rose. This is how Martin Luther explained the meaning of the Luther Seal:

'The just shall live by faith' (Romans 1:17) but by faith in the Crucified. Such a heart should stand in the middle of a white rose, to show that faith gives joy, comfort, and peace. In other words, it places the believer into a white, joyous rose, for this faith does not give peace and joy like the world gives (John 14:27). That is why the rose should be white and not red, for white is the color of the spirits and the angels (cf. Matthew 28:3; John 20:12). Such a rose should stand in a sky-blue field, symbolizing that such joy in spirit and faith is a beginning of the heavenly future joy, which begins already, but is grasped in hope, not yet revealed. And around this field is a golden ring, symbolizing that such blessedness in Heaven lasts forever and has no end. Such blessedness is exquisite, beyond all joy and goods, just as gold is the most valuable, most precious and best metal. ... May Christ, our beloved Lord, be with your Spirit until the life hereafter Amen." (http://www.lutheransonline.com/)

In another recent dream I was on an errand for the church. I was asked to pick up something important that was needed. I drove a long way to my destination and stopped at a beautiful Roman Catholic Church and school. There were young girls lined up, two by two, outside the church wearing white communion dresses with veils on their head. I walked through a door on the side of the church and spoke to someone who appeared to be a priest with a French accent. He asked for identification and what I would like. I told him the name of my church and that I was sent to pick something up. He said I know your pastor he is my friend and it is very important for you to tell him something. He then said, about three times; "It is very important that we have an "ecumenical meeting. Please don't forget to tell him that we need to have an ecumenical meeting." I said "yes I will tell him".

This is an inspiration for re-formation of our oneness. There is only one God, one religion and one spirituality. There are many names and methods of worship for only One Divine Being who is God. We seriously require an ecumenical encounter. Renewal and re-formation of belief systems to include love and peace for all people is a way back to the peace that is of God. This requires increasing insight that promotes unity and resolving of differences. It is necessary to find a satisfactory solution to the separation between God's children. The definition of ecumenical is universal, the worldwide Christian church or unity of all religions. Our purpose is to find a place in the light of God, and be free to live in the present where all are one in God. We are all justified through faith in the One God of Love for All.

Meditative prayer leads to a quiet mind where there is total peace and unity. During this restful state of mind and body, we learn to love and care for all, regardless of religion or belief, as a brother and sister, friend and child. There is a sacred connection with God and all of creation within your mind, heart and soul. We find within the heart of God sacred truth. One day many years ago, I experienced a brief moment of total, universal unconditional Love. I was sitting with a group of friends in a restaurant where we went for dinner when suddenly and for no apparent reason I felt complete and total love for everyone. Maybe it was a moment of insanity but it was an ecstatic feeling. It wasn't just love for friends but for mankind and all that exists. This beautiful sensation was very brief but had a long lasting effect. For a brief moment I understood God's Love because I also felt that I was included in that sense of total sacred love.

Holy insight increases as we meditate and listen for the word of God. This is a way toward awareness of God's Kingdom on earth as it is in Heaven. This is a place where we learn to love and be at peace with all of God's creation. As we move deeper into the universal inner mind, we reach a level of Sacred Spiritual consciousness. Holy insight and discerning is a result of closeness to God's Holy Spirit. Life would be lacking in meaning and purpose if it were completely pre-planned. Loving choices and caring for all people are a necessary function in spiritual growth. We have an ecumenical mission. We are justified by faith and trust that God Loves and cares for all of Creation. God is One, Universal and Cosmic. The Christ personifies this universal God. If we research the history of all religions and beliefs, the whole truth is revealed; that is, all are connected.

Bonding at higher levels of awareness is an evolution in consciousness that is part of God's plan for creation. It is a divine mission to return with the peace, love and compassion that is found in uniting with our beloved creator. We awaken the faculty of insight when entering meditative prayer. Focus, is one of genuine Holy Love as we become aware of the inner self who is one with the Creator. This state of being leads to Spiritual harmony and togetherness for all people. It is imperative now to know that all are one in Love. Awaken and see clearly, as we pray and meditate on the communion of God's Children.

Each vision or dream is an awakening into a spiritual place within a realm of Holy goodness. The meaning may be obvious or deeply hidden. Information related to mental images functions on an instinctive level and affects behavior, outlooks and healing. Behavior and feelings frequently relate to information within the mind of which we are unaware. The insight and information that is received during meditative prayer will help to resolve and change events of the past, present and future. God's time is an eternal and everlasting presence.

Inner vision leads to the grace to view God's reality in a way that leads to Holy guidance. Inspiring prayer for love and unity presented to the mind, produce a current of spiritual power. God is only good. Therefore, profound reflection will renew an entire pattern of understanding. Good thoughts cause good feelings and spiritual living. Mental prayer and images that lead to a quiet mind promotes bonding within the Love of God for all people. Oneness is of God. "You shall love the Lord your God with all your heart, and with all your soul, and with all your mind.' This is the great and foremost commandment. The second is like it, 'You shall love your neighbor as yourself." (Matthew 22:37-39) (1)

Sacred Justification

Pray for guidance and then rest, knowing that God is guiding and caring for you. Visualize yourself protected and guided by The Holy Light of God. Prayer leads to peaceful feelings and inner healing of your mind, body and soul. Just relax in the stillness and quiet of Holy peace. Now image yourself in a picturesque delightful place in nature. This is a spiritual sanctuary for your soul where you are safe and protected by God's Holy Light. It is a place of substance where you have the ability to create. Feel a gentle breeze as it carries the fragrance of the sweet flowers. Listen to the sounds of nature, the birds singing, and the wind blowing through the trees. View the flowers, trees, and the green grass. Blossoms of many colors are falling from flowering trees. The sky is clear and blue with glowing white clouds in the distance. There is a crystal clear stream peacefully stirring a gentle flow of water over a foundation of shimmering pebbles and rocks.

Rest your mind and body and focus on the Holy Spirit of God with you to guide and protect. Starting from the top of your head, slowly move your center of attention and focus on a healing light filling each part of your body and soothing your mind. Let this gentle flow of relaxation continue to move. Feel a soothing wave of lightness as though you are lifting through the air.

Breathe in deeply and exhale slowly. Imagine the air filling your body and spreading relaxation throughout your entire being. With each breath, become calmer. Imagine your body floating upward. Continue moving gently as though above the clouds. In this place, of inner healing, only good, pleasant, thoughts' ideas and feelings can be of any influence. A field of God light protects you and fills your entire being with healing spiritual energy. Quiet your mind of all thought for a moment. Within your mind all that exists is right now. Let all your awareness; focus on a place directly in front of your eyes. A glowing light is forming. As you observe this event, the vision of this Holy Light remains in focus in front of your closed eyes. As you gaze at this beautiful Light it gradually continues to move forward until you see it in front of your closed eyes. Now envision this light expanding to encircle your entire being. This is the Holy Light of God. This is a place of clear vision, within your mind.

A feeling of peacefulness and love fills your mind, heart and soul. The Light of God surrounds you. Only good and loving thoughts or feelings will guide you. As you gaze into this place, your inner mind can review and investigate any situation in your life. Your insight increases gradually, or it may be a sudden realization that becomes evident, as you view your life from a distance. You are calm and peaceful.

The Holy Spirit of God conveys a precise picture of a situation. Understand and revise any misconception accurately. You have the power to transform anything in this picture into a healing event as you have faith and trust that God loves and is caring, for you, and all your needs. You are filled with the peace and grace of God. Peaceful, happy thoughts and feelings replace any difficulty leading to inner healing of your mind, soul, and body.

As you reach your destination, there is a flow of clear vision. Your consciousness is increased and that sense of awareness within your mind extends toward God's Holy Light. As you are embraced by the Light of God, you grow stronger. The power of God brings justification in a perfect way just for you. You are peaceful, content, and in control of all circumstances. This gateway is helping to instill insight, peace and love. The Light of God is an immediate foundation for healing any situation according to God's perfect will. Return to this place at any time to clarify a situation by focusing your attention on the Holy Light of God as your guide. Sacred Love fills your mind, heart and soul through the Grace of God. Love, faith and trust is a sacred gateway to justification.

21. Inner Reflection of God's Holy Presence

A kind and loving soul creates a glow of inner beauty that is outwardly visible. The goodness and light that is part of the soul is a visible and clear reflection of inner beauty. Inner reflection reveals our connection with the Holy Presence of God. Focus, during meditative prayer, on Holy guidance and love leads to inner peace. We live within God's Holy presence in this the moment. Inner reflection on the Holy Presence of God leads to truly knowing and understanding our self as a beautiful creation and child of God. This reflection of the genuine self creates a vision of living in the Spirit of God. As we quiet our mind, there is entrance to a place of peace and goodness. There is an increase in perception of our true self who is an eternal being and one with the sacred light of God.

The presence of God's Holy Spirit becomes an inner and outer reality. There are various levels of awareness. These include the conscious, subconscious and universal or cosmic level that has a significant influence in life. Our mind connects with the Spirit of God. Bonding with this

Divine and Holy consciousness leads to inner healing. During Meditative prayer, images represent the present reality or an imaginative representation of conditions related to life events. When viewed in the reflected Holy Light of God's will, which is only good, our concept of reality becomes clear and perfect. It is always important to focus attention on God's love and goodness to promote health, blessings and strength. Mental images of a concept or idea become meaningful messages to the mind, soul and body. Images, inspired by prayer and focus on the Light of God, create a reflection of inner beauty. We influence the past, and the future in the present moment along a sacred journey of reflection upon the Holy God Light.

Managing Life events through faith and trust in God will promote a healing environment. This is accomplished as we reflect God's Love upon our internal environment during meditative prayer. Most important is belief in the power of God to care for us always. Inner reflection leads to the transformation of beliefs into action and physical response. Mental and spiritual growth depends on the thoughts and ideas that we believe within the mind. Mental awareness and reflection upon life circumstances lead to healing, confidence and an uplifted self-image by the Grace and Light of God.

Inner Reflection within the Flow of Living

During Meditative prayer you are guided to reflect sacred and Holy Light into the flow of living. It is quiet and safe within this place of blessed peace and reflection. Pray and imagine that you are resting in a beautiful location of Holy Peace. There is awareness of God's exquisite creation. You are listening peacefully to the sounds of nature as you begin to rest your mind and body. Rest comfortably as you enter a place of Divine Holiness. You are guided and protected by God's Holy Spirit as you pray and request guidance. Image within your mind and create a reflection of God's sacred guidance.

With closed eyes, begin to view a path. It is pure white and appears to be unending. This pathway is in a beautiful spiritual place lined with radiant flowers. Turn to the right and realize that this path reaches toward the heavens. Turn to the left and continue to become aware of the limitlessness of this passageway. All is occurring in the present moment along this flow of living. As you transform events in the present, you modify your concept and emotional view of events in your life.

Now move closer to the edge of the path and notice that it appears as a shallow stream of pure clear water that is illuminated with Holy Light. Observe the fluid reflection. Notice that it is moving slowly over snowy white stones glistening with particles of diamond light. Ripples glide endlessly along the pure stream. Continue to view this essence of pure life and notice the mirror image. This is a reflection of your present existence, your present self. Your reflection in the flowing stream reveals that you are glowing and filled with the spiritual light of God. You are loved and protected. The Holy Spirit is there always to guide you.

Listen closely to the gentle movement of the flowing current. It is soothing and peaceful like a mountain stream on a clear day. It is so relaxing that you feel a desire to rest. You are sensing an atmosphere of transcendent stillness, as you become aware that you have the means to move closer to God's Holy and sacred Light.

A small boat becomes visible in the distance. As it floats closer, you notice a lining of a smooth, fluffy fabric. As it stops, step into the boat and recline. It is soft and comfortable. The fabric is smooth like glossy silk. Looking upward, the sky is blue and clear. An aura of protecting Divine light surrounds you. Only the Love and Peace of God will influence you in any way. There are controls in front of you. In the middle is a symbol shaped in the form of a triangle that you may touch for Holy guidance and return to the present moment.

Rest now, feeling completely secure and in control. Touch the lever that will guide you toward events that are most significant in your life. Maintain a peaceful mind, as the boat flows along the stream. Swirling streams of God's Holy light energy move in the surrounding atmosphere. It is so peaceful. As you begin to drift into a restful state of mind, observe that you are moving toward a moment that is helpful and pleasant in a perfect way just for you. Your mind begins to reflect upon your destination. Observe within your mind and pray for sacred guidance. Move deeper into a rested and very peaceful state. There is a sensation of deep stillness and increased awareness reflecting your inner self, in God's perfect way, and according to the Holy Will of God.

Your mind and body are at rest and very calm. Your inner mind is active as you come closer to your destination. Your surroundings are beginning to change. Movement is leading toward an event that is significant in influencing your present circumstances. Look into the water and recognize the reflection of your self during this phase of *existence. You may remain here for a moment and view this phase of your life or continue moving. If desired, observe the situation and fill it with the Light of God through prayer. At any time, you can change events and feelings according to God's goodness and peace. You are in complete control at all times. You are surrounded and protected by God's Holy Spirit.*

When you are ready, return feeling rested and refreshed. Feel wonderful when you return. You understand and are aware of your inner feelings and know that you have the power of inner reflection to resolve any problem and clarify any situation in a perfect way according to the Holy Will of God. You are reflecting the Light of God into your Life.

22. Transforming Care of the Soul

A transforming relationship is one in which we care for another unconditionally without expectation of anything in return for that devoted attention. Caring bestows a spontaneous benefit; as we give we receive in return. This may not always be obvious but it is experienced within the heart, soul and entire being. A caring interaction, given unconditionally, is the creative and transforming Spirit of all life. Extending the love of God to others is an influence for creative peaceful living; that evolves into an advanced form of spirituality. This leads to a conversion of the human soul and a sense of oneness with the divine presence. Unconditional loving care is the creative energy for transforming our mind and soul that leads to inner peace and healing.

As we have understanding for all and envision their spiritual true self, we create a genuine caring relationship. See a reflection of God's goodness in others and realize that all are one in God's plan of living. As we form a sacred connection with another, there is evolution into an advanced level of consciousness and spiritual growth. Unconditional loving care leads to a spiritual awakening.

During meditative prayer imagery, there is creation of God's perfect reality in a discipline of mental prayer that leads to fulfillment and transformation. We then become aware of the connection that exists between those who truly care. Realize this within the mind; where thought becomes reality, and all are accepted and trusted without expectation of benefit. There is satisfaction in the peace that is felt when we give and receive spiritual care with love.

Mind, soul and body function in a bond of loving care. During Mental Prayer, loving and holy images become profound messages to the internal environment of the self. This inner mental prayer experience is reality to the mind. Each word inspires an image that forms a belief. As you learn to accept and love yourself, care for another is a natural response. A peaceful mind and soul is the outcome of concern and compassion. Loving thought is a method of inner healing. You are transforming apprehension into tranquility to promote a life of divine blessings. A transforming bond creates peace and happiness. Caring relationships are the substance for shaping a harmonious life.

Transformational Healing

The peace and love of God our Heavenly Father is with you now, to fill you with blessings and unending peace. Pray for guidance and transforming love. Begin with prayer, rest your body and clear your mind. Ask God to help you to create a loving relationship within your mind. Increase your awareness of all surrounding beauty by creating within your mind a sacred space of holy peace and love. Do this within your mind, as you imagine a location that is pleasant and peaceful. Rest now and increase in awareness of your relationship with all living things. Love for one evolves into heavenly appreciation of all life.

Rest your mind and allow any thoughts to just float by as leaves on a peaceful moving stream. Within your mind, request direction from God, and feel a sense of Holy protection. Receive guidance that flows from God's Holy Spirit. In this state of mental peace only good pleasant thoughts or feelings will influence you. The presence of angelic love and sacred presence encircles and safeguards you. You are in complete charge. Pray for guidance and transforming love. Within your mind review an experience of feeling love for another and receiving love in return. Believe that as you care for another you are caring for the one who you truly love. Now as you experience this sense of Holy Love, you are beginning to enter a state of complete rest within the silence and peace of your mind.

Focus your attention on relaxing the muscles of each part of your body. Slowly move your focus of concentration from the top of your head to the bottom of your feet. Relax your face, neck, arms, hands, and fingers. Let this gentle flow of mellowness continue to move down your legs. Feel a soothing wave of lightheartedness as though merging within the atmosphere.

You are aware of an exceptional pleasant fragrance as you breathe in deeply and exhale slowly. Imagine with each breath that your lungs are filling with a soothing mist. With each breath, your sense of composure is increasing. You are experiencing a place of sharing and togetherness. Just rest each part of your body. Take a moment to do that. Remain in this undisturbed state, avoiding all thought for a few moments. As thoughts begin to enter your mind, just let them pass naturally.

Now imagine lying comfortably near a stream of gently flowing water. The atmosphere is enchanting, as the sun is reflecting sparkling light upon the moving water. There is movement in the surrounding trees as the birds move through the branches and sing calmly. The day is bright and clear. A refreshing sensation fills the atmosphere. With each breath, imagine the air flowing and causing a sense of ease throughout your body. Take a deep breath now and breathe out slowly feeling all the tensions leaving your body. You can continue now breathing easily and becoming more peaceful. Your mind is clear, and receptive. It is like a quiet lakeside, where the silence of the still water is flickering with illumination, as the flowing stream trickles into the lake. You are ready to experience new outcomes as you envision a new and inspirational passage inward.

Continue to rest peacefully. Breathe easily, as you become more at ease, contented, and comfortable with each breath. Your mind is peaceful and calm. This will cause a deep and lasting impression within your mind that will remain for as long as required, in a perfect way just for you. You are moving into a deep peaceful state. Imagine within your mind that you can blend with the wind. Move into a flower or a leaf and sense it from within. Meet with anyone that you like. This is the miraculous ability of your mind and the soul. You can be anywhere or with anyone that you wish in a loving relationship.

Drift easily now, and allow yourself to enjoy this very peaceful, relaxed state of being. Your conscious mind can let go completely. Your inner mind receives and understands all information.

You are filled with God's Spirit of peace and Holy Love. This leads you to understand and care for others in a manner that will bring closeness and peace to all. Your focus is divine and heavenly peace that promotes healing love. You are placing primary concern on the Love of God, yourself and others. This is an important concept in that entering the meditative prayer requires total focus on the present moment and the presence of God. Focus your mind on this moment. You control the circumstances of any situation by your thought that God's Holy Will be done. You are becoming aware of pleasant feeling as you rest and ask for guidance.

Loving kind action within your mind increases your sense of peace and happiness. This type of loving relationship is spiritual in nature. You view others in the form of their spiritual self, which is perfect, beautiful and genuine. You see a reflection of yourself in others and realize that all are one in a scheme of consciousness that is presently beyond imagination. Awareness of this state of consciousness helps to make the flow of life satisfying. As God's healing light flows through your entire being, there is a realization of your connectedness with all creation. You are free to transform any condition, or to remain as you are. Loving relationships are the foundation for happiness and contentment. There is then freedom that reaches beyond time and space. You are one in a caring relationship.

23. Sanctified Perception of Reality

As a young child, I believed that I had the ability to take flight and fly. I dreamed this frequently but perceived it as a reality rather than a dream. In reality I actually did play on a large roof where we lived in New York. I recall that I regularly walked to the edge of the roof and very easily, just lifted up, and flew through the air at will. One day, I lost this ability at a time when there was serious reason for escape. I envisioned a fire encircling the roof. I thought that I should fly above it but I was unable to do so.

Each person has separate and individual perception. We each live in our own private world of personal reality. We need to rediscover how to free the mind and soul from personal human captivity. A soul created to be free and one with God is confined to a human physical body. There is minimal true knowledge of who, what, where and why we exist. I once had a recollection and belief in total freedom without doubt of its reality or question about the purpose of living.

Now in this present moment I have faith, trust and belief in God and the reality that I perceive. This is a sanctified perception of a greater truth but now I will accept the limited and yet sufficient knowledge that is retained within this life. Here and now it seems that we are living in a dream and creating each scene one at a time. What I think I am, that is what I am. Each person views reality differently. I believe in a perfect, beautiful and sanctified world created by God.

Our place of origin is one of perfection. There is a desire for the peace and beauty, which is part of our heritage and soul memory. Creation is only good, perfect and beautiful. The human soul inherently recalls this peaceful sanctuary and longs to return to paradise. An elevation in consciousness is the result of this natural desire for perfection in all phases of living. We are created in the image of God, who is flawless. As we feel contentment our self, there is a sense of serenity. We then move in the direction of living in the Spirit of God where all is peace and contentment. Stillness and silence of the mind leads to sanctification.

Heavenly Blessedness exists on this earth as it is in Heaven. Wellbeing is enhanced and joy fills the mind and soul as we experience a sanctified perception of reality. There is a sense of blending in an atmosphere of Love. There is freedom and control of this life in which all needs are fulfilled. Meditative Prayer leads to an elevation in consciousness to the degree of understanding that there is a higher and greater purpose in living. We have the power to move beyond the ordinary into an atmosphere where consciousness is unlimited. The flow of God's Love brings peace and harmony that leads to awareness of an unlimited potential. This is a Sanctified perception of reality where all are blessed by the Spirit of God.

Sanctified Perception

Rest comfortably now and imagine yourself resting in a place of beauty and perfection. Pray, and know that you are surrounded and protected by the light of God. Colorful flowers and towering trees surround you. There are waterfalls in the distance and the sound of running water as it rushes into the sea. The ocean water is bright blue green as the sun shines and creates a glimmer of pure white sparkling bubbles of water.

Abide in Love the Sacred Presence of God

As you rest, imagine the ocean flowing into rivers and streams. Move now into a very deep state of relaxation where a sense of goodness and peace flows into your consciousness clearly and pleasingly. Continue to enter that place within your mind of infinite intelligence and sanctity. You are always in control and guided by God's Holy Spirit.

As you view this vision of natural beauty and perfection, your soul will reach a blessed and dearly loved destination. This sanctified perception of reality is that place where love is abundant and there is a sense of attunement with all living things. It is the beauty of nature filling all objects with pure animation in a world of unlimited goodness. As you rest in this place of natural radiance, you are receiving a sacred flow of the Holy Love of God.

Imagine a beam of pure sanctified and holy light. This is the light of God. Request guidance and visualize this inner light as you relax each muscle of your body. Feel yourself, becoming completely at ease. Breathe in through your nose and out through your mouth. With each breath, focus on a stream of Sacred Light moving through the center of your body. You are totally protected by the Holy Spirit of God and only good will influence you in any way. Sense a gentle vibration. There is a sensation of total and complete relaxation. You are always in control.

Now within your mind you may go anywhere that you wish. Feel yourself, floating. You may envision yourself in a special place where you are peaceful and happy or move into the atmosphere and glide with the clouds. You are receiving inner guidance by the Holy Spirit of God and realize that total control is your decision. From this place, you see from a distance all phases of life and understand the meaning and purpose of each situation.

It is so pleasant and peaceful to realize that the flow of God's Life Spirit is filling your entire being. Your thoughts, and guidance of God's Holy Spirit, control every move. Return now to where you are free and aware of the flow of life. Return to the present reality knowing that you have the ability to be free, happy and peaceful at all times. Your perception of reality is sanctified. Rest in the Silence and peace.

24. Flow of Spirit for Life

The following describes a vivid dream state. "In a dream, I was standing with a friend at the oceanfront. He was fishing and pulled in a large beautiful fish. It was an exquisite color in shades of deep blue green and approximately three feet long. Gentle fins around the head were waving in the wind. The eyes were bright and clear and conveyed a loving sensation. I felt as though I was able to communicate with the fish mentally as we made eye contact. There was a sense of oneness as though we were of one infinite spirit. The fish was hanging and then lowered to the ground. I said, do not hurt it. It is so beautiful. My friend said, all right, we will keep it. The scene changed and I walked toward my friend who showed me that the fish is living in a small pool of water. I said it would soon die in there. It has no room to swim and move and it is not getting enough oxygen from this small amount of water. As I turned, we were facing a lake. My friend said we could let the fish go into the lake. I thought that this was not what it needed since it came from the Ocean, but it was better than being in the small pool. I picked up the fish and held it sensing a strong connection between us. I carried the fish to the lake and put it into the water. The lake then transformed into an ocean with huge blue green waves, as the fish moved toward the water. A wind blew and a wave swept the fish toward shore and on to the beach. My friend called to me and said you can help. I ran across the beach, removing one shoe and one sock at a time I ran. There was a sensation of freedom as I picked up the fish and glided effortlessly toward the ocean. The fish slipped into the ocean and at this moment, I became aware that I was free and alive in the flow of life." (3)

This dream occurred approximately ten years ago. It is written in my first book "Valley of the Silent Stream." I didn't realize then how prophetic it is. Separation from our true identity with God is similar to being a fish out of water. Great love and compassion leads us to return to our home in an ocean of unity with each other and God. It appears as a long journey but at times seems like a flash in a dream. Love, empathy and understanding is a guide that directs our soul in the direction of freedom.

I saw beauty and felt love and compassion, as I looked into the green sparkling eyes of the fish. There was a sense of sadness in its eyes and yet a message was being conveyed. This is a living creature and creation of God. There was an expression of feeling that extended from this beautiful creation. I realized that we are one in the Holy Spirit of God. As I released the fish into the ocean, I was free. We must let go in order to be free. It is a combined act of love of self, and yet letting go of yourself that brings peace and freedom.

Freedom is achieved through genuine empathy and understanding. This leads to an individual who will act freely, is living in the present and is in the process of spiritual growth. It is the use of empathetic understanding, which penetrates the inner reality in order to understand and comprehend the feelings of another. A sense of freedom involves becoming aware of self as an individual who is part of all.

There is a special purpose for your life, and every form of life. It is the perfection of creation unflawed by selfishness. The self has developed its personal self-nature and expands to include all. We are moving in the direction of conscious evolution of the soul in the Holy Spirit of God.

You are a Spiritual Being, moving toward, living in the Spirit of God.

I thought of this dream today during a sermon in church in which the pastor talked about a man who dreamed of a beautiful fish and felt love and compassion. I believe that God is telling me something important. I did not connect the fish with the symbol of Christianity, which is a fish, for ten years. Jesus Christ and multiple world religious and spiritual teachings focus on the importance of Love and compassion for all. We merge into a universal sea of infinite love and compassion and live in the Spirit of God's Peace when we realize that all are one in the Love of God.

Flow of Life Giving Spirit

Pray for guidance and rest in a comfortable position where you will be uninterrupted and at peace. Clear your mind of all thought. Feel yourself in a place of peace and contentment. Within your mind, you are unlimited; you possess the power to be anywhere that you wish. Create an image within your mind of your personal safe retreat. Relax each part of your body, starting from the top of your head. Become aware of the muscles in your face. Sense any tightness and then consciously focus on resting each muscle.

Breathe in deeply and exhale slowly. With each breath, sense a peaceful loving presence beginning to surround your entire being. Now let the muscles in your neck relax. Feel the muscles in your neck relaxing completely. Let your shoulder muscles rest now. There is a sense of lightness as you release any heaviness or tightness in your shoulder area. As you continue to breathe normally, the Holy Light of God moves through your entire being. Your mind and body is resting completely. A gentle sensation of peace, love, and protection surrounds your entire existence. Only good thoughts, ideas or feelings can influence you in any way.

Breathe in deeply and exhale slowly. Imagine the air filling with a soothing vapor. With each breath, become more serene and calm. Imagine a journey to a place of serenity and comfort. Envision yourself, floating and moving toward that place. Move gently forward and begin to glide silently toward your destination. It is so pleasant to sense the soothing gently breeze, as you move toward your destination. Just continue moving and become more peaceful as you rest and sense the freedom. Your mind is now in a place of stillness. Any thought is just drifting by easily. Let your mind remain clear of all thought and quietly wait for inner guidance. Take a few moments to do that as you remain in the present moment.

Your sense of satisfaction and connection with all increases as you continue to rest. You are experiencing a sense of total perfect blending, of mind and body, within the nature of God and all life. Your sacred awareness is increasing. Feel and understand your connection with all existence. Become aware of the beauty and perfection in every living thing and all of nature. Understand that a spiritual connection binds one to another in an atmosphere of sacred love. You may return to this place of mental peace at any time by just closing your eyes and imaging the light entering your mind and body. This flow of Spirit for Life, is God's creation. You are entering God's Kingdom on this earth.

25. Spiritual Healing

Spiritual healing is integrated into the process of Meditative Prayer. We have the ability to pray for the healing creative energy of God to flow through us. This loving interaction produces a spiritual atmosphere of loving care. The forces that surround the human body are an extension of the individual. We touch and heal, by the power of God, moving through the Human soul. This power belongs to the Holy Spirit of God. The gift of healing is bestowed by the Holy Spirit. It is a concept that is part of an ancient knowledge.

All science, technology, art and all that is good, are a creation within the mind of God. Mind and body respond harmoniously to the healing Touch of God. Mind with all its abilities, and connection with God, is universal and eternal. It is a spark of God's infinite intelligence that promotes spiritual healing. When God's Spiritual creative energy is focused in a loving and harmonious way, vital centers of the body activate in a manner that causes this loving intension to extend healing to others. The evolution of the mind is part of the evolution of the soul. It is a birth in spirit.

Closeness, and the human loving touch, causes your inner self to feel accepted and connected with God and all humanity. It is a cause of joy and healing. Your life giving needs are then satisfied. Each has a different interpretation and idea concerning life. A sense of inner healing occurs as you rest your mind and body to receive the Healing Light of God. You accomplish this through prayer and a silent mind.

Spiritual Healing begins within the mind of God, where images evolve into reality. As you rest your mind and body and think kind and loving thoughts, you become a channel of divine healing power. This is something that all require in their span of living. Love creates a need and desire to help and heal. When there is someone whom you truly feel love for, this power becomes stronger and more powerful. You then know without question that love, which is the Love of God, generates power for healing.

Healing in the Holy Spirit of God

Pray for Holy Guidance. Ask that the Holy Spirit be your Guide as you pray and meditate. Believe and have faith that you are safe and protected by the loving Holy Spirit of God. Only good that flows from God will influence you in any way. The Spirit of God is with you always. You are one in spirit and sacred love.

Focus your thoughts on the Holy Presence of God. Expectation and trust in the power of God to provide a perfect solution to any problem, causes a blessed state of peace. Rest as you sense the serenity of this Holy perception. Rest your mind and body. Starting from the top of your head, slowly move your focus of concentration and rest each part of your body. Let this gentle flow of a peaceful loving feeling embrace you. You are embraced in the arms of God.

Breathe in deeply and exhale slowly. Feel the air fresh and vitalizing. With each breath, experience the sense of serenity. Continue to feel peaceful and comfortable. Your mind is accepting only good Holy guidance and feelings. There is awareness of total protection by the loving presence of God as you begin to contemplate what your inner mind will communicate.

Abide in Love the Sacred Presence of God

Begin to become aware now of the knowledge that your mind has been receiving. Intricate information has been filling your inner mind since your soul was created. You possess great wisdom, far beyond your conscious awareness. This wisdom is part of your development. It is a Holy gift of God that is available for your benefit.

A light in the distance begins to become increasingly more visible. It is getting stronger and clearer. Within this Holy, guiding and protective Light of God, review now any circumstances that may be causing uncertainty. Observe from a distance as though you are viewing a play and become aware of a solution that will lead to resolving any difficulty in a perfect way according to God's will. Mentally restructure any information in a manner that is helpful for you, and then forgive unconditionally and with love. Remember the words recollection, mental renewal, and unconditional loving forgiveness. These words lead to unity and inner peace. Take a moment to do that now as you continue to relax and be at peace.

There is a wonderful feeling now of peace in knowing that a sense of inner unity and quiet focus is helping you. Certainty and confidence are part of your character. You are gaining knowledge that will expand your abilities and provide the means to use your God-given ability wisely. You have the power and ability to interact with others in a manner that extends creative energy for healing.

You are a channel of love, a channel of peace, a channel of healing. You are a caring and loving person. Receive now the Holy Light of God, let it move through your entire being. Within your mind, think of someone whom you would like to help and send healing prayer with love. Focus the Light of God through your body and into your hands. Within your mind, send healing prayer and light to the one who you wish to help. Take a few moments now in silent contemplation and prayer as you focus on the Healing Light of God. Return feeling wonderful, peaceful, rested and renewed. You have received all that you require to be a blessing to those in need.

26. Unity in the Holy Spirit

Unity is a sense of oneness in thinking, feeling, and understanding. It is the ability to put our self in the place of another. There is a connection or loving bond that develops between people. We understand what the other is feeling and can convey that sense of empathy. It is essential to establish a sense of unity and peace between all people. The ability to put our self in the other person's place and to feel with another is important in all relationship. There is no obvious way to determine the true feelings of another. It is necessary to accept without question the verbal expression of feeling by another. Unity leads to understanding that there is a reasonable cause for all emotion. Unity starts when we knowingly resolve to feel with another person. "What you say you feel, I believe and understand because we are one in spirit and love." (3) When we trust and care with unconditional love, each will be healed in a way that is God's perfect will. This is the beginning of a true healing relationship.

We always maintain a personal sense of self in that we become a source of strength for another. We are in control of our own feelings and let the Light of God be our guide with trust that the situation will be resolved in a perfect way according to the will of God. Caregivers must maintain their own strength in order to help another. Peacefulness, calm and confidence are essential for healing. Clear thinking with intelligence and knowledge requires a peaceful mind.

Peace and a unified understanding of each person's beliefs and motivation is an important and necessary component for life. Separation between people due religion or spiritual beliefs is completely contrary to God's Divine plan and intension. Unconditional love for all people is vital for life. We are to Love One Another. This is the Will of God. There is only one God for all people and yet there is incalculable separation in belief systems. It is imperative now that the unity is realized. We are a unified creation of One Holy and Divine God. Our sense of focus and creativity increases as we become aware of belonging to each other and God. This leads to peace and universal cosmic healing.

Inner strength improves when communication is directed in a loving manner. Caring words that convey unity in thought have an effect within the deepest segments of the mind. A gesture of kindness that shows concern and caring is as healing as any medical treatment. A sense of connection and care leads to universal healing. We are then free of difficulty and have a sense of security in our environment.

Outstanding strength in personality begins with unity. Good loving thought transforms. To heal is to make whole. A whole is one. Division is weak and scattered. We are to establish a reciprocal relationship that is favorable and healing to all concerned. We always receive in return that which is given to others. The result is inner healing transmitted to all with God's Love.

Practice of the art of meditative prayer causes a flow of God's Holy Spirit, which expands in a way that we can direct it in a loving and healing manner. Merging within the Light of God is a form pure love leading to an elevation in consciousness. This is a Healing vibration in the course of Human existence. This is the ultimate phase of discovery and understanding. Inner guidance leads to that silent place within the mind where connection with the Divine transpires. This restructures our discernment and awareness.

We then clear our mind and heart of concern and learn to Love One Another. It is the beginning of unification. Harmony is the result. Love that emanates from within our heart and soul can free us. There is unity with God, our divine origin, and all creation. Movement toward the Light of God as we reach out to others, in a gesture of affection, leads to peace. We may use this energy with reverence. It is a spiritual connection of our soul one to another and God.

Unity in the Spirit of God

Pray and imagine yourself in very special and sacred place. This is a place of Love and Holy protection where you are peaceful and secure. Only good exists in God's reality. Within your mind, thought instantly creates the object of your belief. Relax there appreciating the stillness and serenity. See, feel and listen with a sense of enhanced mindfulness. Conceive within your mind a visualization and belief of perfect unity with love and caring. Imagine a healing light within your body, mind, and soul. You are a perfect creation in every way and each day your inner mind is working to uphold that perfect creation.

Look into a mirror within your mind and create your perfect self. Imagine a flawless mirror duplicate of yourself. Notice your hair, your eyes, your nose and your mouth. Let all the muscles in your body relax completely. See, hear, and feel yourself exactly the way that you wish to be. Envision your perfect self. Design a mental image of your body, mind and soul. See your perfect situation, your character and your spiritual purpose. Take a few moments to do that.

You are responsible for your life. Believe in the good and the beautiful in all of creation and all of God's people. Trust in the perfection and innocence of all. See, feel, and hear the value in all things. The only reality is absolute love. All adversity is a creation of the human mind. Focus on seeing only the good. All of creation is good.

Within your mind envision yourself in a beautiful forest. Recognize the sense of perfection, majesty, and vastness. It is a clear day and you see a glistening lake nearby. The water is so pure that you can see to the bottom of the lake. There is a reflection of yourself upon the water. Notice yourself, as a perfect mirror image. Walk to the water and merge in spirit with that perfect image of your spiritual self. The Holy Spirit of God is with you to guide and protect. Create a vision of unity with your true self and all creation.

This is the water of life and the stream of infinite consciousness. Walk peacefully toward a waterfall and view the peaceful flowing water. Inner healing of your mind, body and soul transpires in a perfect way. Let go now of any concern. This healing water promotes peace and self-confidence to understand your oneness and connection with all. You now have the ability to accept and give spiritual love freely without reservation. Believe and know that you are a kind and good person who deserves this sense of unity with all. You feel calm, happy and fulfilled as you return feeling wonderful in every way. There is a place of healing love within you.

27. The Presence of Guardian Angels

"Angel of God, my guardian dear, to whom God's Love commits thee here. Forever and this day be at my side, to light and guard, to rule and guide." (2)

Angels appear in many forms and in in all areas of life. We may not recognize their presence but the result is clear. A few years ago I was riding in the car with a friend. I was in the seat next to him. I usually watch the road but I began to feel tired and fell into a partial half awake and half asleep state. I closed my eyes, and suddenly felt a child who was about two years kneeling on my lap and facing me. He poked my cheek with his little fingers and said, "Stay awake, don't go to sleep". He then disappeared and I was wide awake. Within a short time, I noticed that the car was going off the road down a hill and headed toward a wall. It should have taken less than a second to hit the wall at the speed that we were going but time slowed down. I had time to think about what was happening. I noticed and realized that the driver was sleeping. I called for him to wake up. He heard me call, woke up quickly and immediately turned the wheel toward the road. We were then back on the road and on our way. The side of the car was scraped but we were well and alive. I believe that I was awakened by an Angel who saved our life. My only explanation is our Guardian Angel was with us.

I believe this to be a miraculous event. These episodes occur every day throughout the world. At times, they may seem insignificant. We look for rational explanations but the final answer is beyond logical comprehension. Many angelic visitations appear as a normal event. Persons who truly care with love are performing with angelic guidance. Miraculous interventions occur regularly. You are never alone these heavenly beings materialize to help, heal, protect and guide.

We have guardian angels with us always. They are our inner guides and messengers of God's Holy Light. One, who is an instrument of healing, creates an angelic healing space within their self that, will enhance the opportunity for another person to feel secure and safe in their environment. They are the earths Angels and they are my Angels. They are sent by God. We help others by conveying genuine concern and caring, expressing kindness and understanding of the needs of each individual. A gentle touch and the extending of your hand in recognition of deeds of kindness leads to inner peace and healing. You are receiving guidance from the Angels of God your guardian.

Awareness of the Presence of Angels

Rest and pray for the presence of God's Heavenly Guardian Angels. Focus on the center of love, which comes from your heart. Feel a sense of peace in the knowledge of oneness with God's Love and all creation. This causes joy and maintains goodness and peace in your life. All are one in God's Love. We are sisters and brothers, like leaves on one tree of life. We are part of the tree and it is part of us. We are children of God. You are finding the love that you seek as you realize that an angelic heart is part of you.

Clear your mind and let your eyes close naturally. Avoid all conscious thought just let any thought float by as on a peaceful stream. Focus on your heart and breathe in and out deeply and slowly. Think of someone who you love or have loved. Focus on the feeling of love in your heart and soul. Let the Light of Holy Love move throughout your entire body. Now allow the Light within your heart to extend upward and grow stronger until you sense the light and peace within your mind. Be there for a moment and remain in the presence of this moment.

As you focus on this divine light filling your heart and mind, allow the light to rise up through the crown of your head. Envision this Holy Light extending toward the heavens and merging in the Light of God and your Guardian Angels. Pray and ask for guidance and inner vision of your Sacred Angels. Envision God's Holy angels and ask that they always be with you to help, to heal to guide and to protect. Receive the gift of faith and trust that you are eternally loved and cared for. May you always be guided, protected and cared for by the Angels of God. Remain in silent communion now and receive God's inspiration and Guidance as your guardian angels speak to you within your soul and inner being.

28. Spiritual Union

Divine love is part of God's Holy plan of life. The Kabbalah, an ancient Jewish mystical tradition based on an esoteric interpretation of the Old Testament, teaches that, if we are worthy of it, we will share life together with our soulmate not just in this temporal world but for all eternity. The soul whose time has come for it to enter into this world separates into two halves one half in the male and one half in the female. When these two halves meet again in their original association, the bond of heavenly love returns.

Twin souls, are believed to be the other half of our soul. Each person has one twin, and after being split by God the two went their separate ways. Each twin is a complete soul, it is their mission to increase in wholeness and become enlightened, before reunification with each other and God. This reunion is of two complete and whole beings. According to ancient wisdom, when a soul is born or incarnated from God, it is created in a group. The souls in this group are our soulmates, they are very similar in character. Each of these souls is split into two, creating the twins. According to tradition and ancient beliefs the soul will experience many incarnations or rebirth into life before reunion with its twin soul and ascension to God.

Part of this Jewish tradition is reincarnation which is mentioned throughout the texts of Jewish mysticism, including the Kabbalah and the Zohar. Reincarnation is the reentry of the soul into an entirely new body into the present world. Resurrection, by contrast, is the reunification of the soul with the former body (newly reconstituted) into a new world. The purpose of reincarnation is either to make up for problems in the former life or to create a new, higher state of perfection. According to Christian doctrine, if the soul is not ready for Heaven, it will go to purgatory until worthy to enter Heaven and reunification with God. There are many varied and conflicting beliefs related to the afterlife and eternity. The true reality is only in the present moment. Time and space is only of the earth and our concept of life. God's reality is the eternal presence of this moment. We are eternal beings living in the presence of God. Our mission is to awaken and become conscious of our true self.

Within each of us is a sense of spiritual belonging. There is a twin presence in all forms of life. According to ancient beliefs, in a desire for companionship, the self-divided to create another who would be the perfect partner. These divisions are the impelling forces of the soul. As each soul divided, an individual person came into existence. The human soul desires to return to this soul from whom it separated. Reunion leads to spiritual love. You regain part of yourself and increase in wholeness. This is reunification within the Holy Spirit of God. The self will extend its consciousness and remain aware of its self as an individual. You mature in mind, body, spirit and soul as you reach that level of perfect love.

Awakening to the Light of God brings about balance and wholeness. We are in touch with God's eternal loving presence. We sense this love in the person of another and all who we love. This is a connection with the lost beloved who is God and the foundation of all love. When embraced in the heart of this divine love we are in rapture. We are in communion within the Love of God. This love includes all creation, our twin, angel and special friend who always lives within our mind and heart, and is always there for us. This is the nature of God incarnate in all creation. During meditative prayer we reach a mystical level of consciousness where we become aware of the love that lives within. This love is eternal, we are together forever.

The true beloved is God and the love of God. During meditative prayer our focus is on silence and being in God's Holy presence. We are to Love God above all the things of heaven and earth. Love of God includes love of all. Let the Holy Spirit be our one and only guide. God is one. Now we are going to eliminate duality and grow in spirit and truth leading to wholeness. Our true purpose and focus is reunion with our God and Creator through grace and the sanctification of the soul.

In Teresa's book: The Life of Saint Teresa of Jesus, she says: This spark "seems to ... Rise from the ashes. ... They shall mount up with wings like eagles, they shall run and not be weary, Teresa says, "You will have read certain books on prayer which advise the soul to enter within itself: and that is exactly what this means." The Rapture of the Soul, Teresa says, "One kind of rapture is this." The soul is yearning for God and He "is moved with compassion". Then, we become like the phoenix that "catches fire and springs into new life." She says, the soul is cleansed and "God unites it with Himself, in a way which none can understand save it and He". (The Interior Castle: Sixth Mansions: Chapter Four) (18)

Healing through Spiritual Union

Pray that God's Holy Love and Peace is with you. Rest your mind and body. Breathe in deeply and exhale slowly. With each breathe, you are more peaceful and serene. Now, just be there in the silence, and know that you are in a safe place of sacred peace and love. Rest quietly and pray, within your mind, that the Loving Presence of God is with you. As you pray, become aware of the silence and focus on God's Holy Spirit. This is a silent and sacred place. Only goodness and love exists. This Love is beyond imagination and explanation.

There is a sense of joining in an atmosphere of Holy and pure Love. The spirit, mind and soul blend in an environment of loving peace and acceptance. There is the sensation of being held and embraced by the Holy Spirit of Love. There is a flow of movement as waves in an ocean of particles that extend loving affection within the Light of God. Only goodness exists in this sanctified place. Remain in the silence and repeat within your mind "The Holy and Sacred Love of God, is with me now and always. I devote my life and soul to You Dear Lord God." I ask to be united in the Holy Spirit of Your Love, my God. I ask for forgiveness and I forgive all. Bring me closer to you. Be with me now and always.

Rest now in the silence. Avoid thought, just be there and listen. Receive inspiration and accept the Holy Love of God. Let go of your sense self as a separate being and unite with the Sanctified Love of the Creator. Be there now, surrounded, protected and filled with Holy Love. This is a Spiritual Union and a sacred healing of the mind, heart and soul. As we love one another with a pure and unconditional love, God is there with us. There is union with our long lost love for whom we are searching through eternity. The members of our spiritual family sense God's Holy presence and find their way home like a magnet drawn to its opposite pole. We are on the way to living in the Spirit of God.

29. A Compassionate Spirit

"He "is moved with compassion". Then, we become like the phoenix that "catches fire and springs into new life." the soul is cleansed and "God unites it with Himself, in a way which none can understand save it and He". (18)

In a therapeutic relationship, caring is more important than knowing. The best medical knowledge is insignificant without a caring heart to use that knowledge with love and wisdom. One who cares is truly working with God in a healing alliance. The Heart of God is compassionate and extends healing love to all people. All of God's creation is justifiable and worthy of receiving this restorative devotion.

During meditative prayer, within the mind, there is the ability to reach out and touch another with healing Spiritual Love in a way that flows from God's Holy Spirit. This requires a caring loving heart and commitment to the Love of God. The compassionate Spirit of God is nurturing, kind and caring. One who cares is guided toward compassion and love for all.

There is, then, the ability to freely experience the presence of God in our Life. A caring heart has the initiative and Holy guidance that is essential to work jointly, in an empathetic association for spiritual care. Concern and compassion for another is a necessary part of the process of healing.

Immeasurable understanding fills our mind and soul as we approach another with empathy and understanding for their needs. Spiritual care with love reveals to all the power of God's Holy guidance. You are a spiritual channel of help and healing to another. You create a network of power, energy and love. The only effective method of restoration to health is caring with true concern. This comprises complete commitment and understanding of the one that you wish to help. A spiritual care giver, whose heart is truly concerned, will communicate a sense of supportive action. This act of love produces a spiritual bond, which inspires the other to heal and restores health to your body, heart, soul and mind.

Extending one's self in a loving relationship causes an awareness of feelings that once were dormant. There is a sense of confidence and self-awareness. Devotion to another, and the Holy Love of God that it communicates, leads to a Blessed relationship within the Light of God. We learn to see all as a reflection God's Light in this affectionate bond.

Compassion in the Spirit of God

Help us Dear Lord to Love each other; to understand and to care about the needs and beliefs of each person. Receive this inspiration now. In order to live in the Spirit of God, believe and have faith. There is One God for all people throughout the universal plan of creation. Closeness to the Holy Spirit requires only Love. God is Love. God is one with all, in all languages and with all people. Image the One God in every belief that, at its fundamental teaching, inspires Love for all. If you say to another "you must follow this teacher, this prophet, this Holy One or Enlightened One", (1) you are inviting togetherness with in you. You believe that you are helping another to come closer to the True God who is in and with us eternally.

Rest now pray and visualize within your mind images of beauty and perfection. There is a field of flowers, colored in every rainbow hue glistening as the sun shines on each blossom. The clouds in the distance are moving slowly and changing form. As you notice them, fading and reforming you feel a sense of oneness with all that surrounds you. Become aware of a feeling peace and let the loving Light of God fill your mind, heart and soul. This pure sacred light is entirely revitalizing your total being. You are peaceful and calm as you focus on this touch of loving care. Just rest peacefully and let go totally. You are filled and protected by the blessed Light of God.

Become aware of an aura of sacred loving presence surrounding your body. As it, flows from the heavens, its focus centers around your heart. There is an understanding of commitment and love which is an essential component of life. This is compassion, caring and true concern. The understanding of togetherness changes into an eternity, which removes any concern of separation from this sense of compassionate love.

It is bright and clear as you reflect upon a stream of clear flowing water. There is awareness of all existence, unending and perfect. The flow is gentle, like waves in an ocean of warm fluid, tender, protecting and bonding one to another; you are creating a sense of connection and sacred caring. There is the sensation of a loving stream including all in a human bond. In this bonding of ourselves, we are in touch with genuine love. There is awareness, giving special meaning to your life. Something that was once lost has returned. You understand the nature of caring feelings. It is an awakening from a dream, in which all was vague, and now the reality of your being is apparent. When compassionate love and caring for another is unconditional, each is blessed by the spirit of God. Life is new and beautiful. All is seen in the light of God's compassion and goodness. All of nature becomes alive with brilliance and sanctified vision. A gentle breeze causes a movement in the trees. As you feel, see and hear life moving within the atmosphere, you know the presence of a living God. This Love is oneness with God's presence, and each other.

There is an effortless sense of understanding between you and another; your thinking communicates the significance that, I care for you because you are you. Your happiness is my happiness. Your life is my life. As you think, I think, as you feel I feel. I have my own life and desires, but I believe that as I feel, you feel. I as care, you care. If I am happy, you are happy. Oneness of spirit indicates that two think and feel with understanding and empathy for the other and live within the compassionate Love of God.

30. Serenity of the Soul

You are a beautiful and perfect creation of God. In the beginning God created man and woman and placed them in a beautiful garden of eternal peace and serenity. They were given free will but asked to live according to the will of God the creator. Failure to do so leads to a natural response according to the design of creation. Each object in nature is divinely good when used according to the creators plan. Deviation from Gods exquisite design leads us away from God. Home in paradise was soon lost. Free will led to chaos and loss of serenity.

God created this beautiful earth. There is water which gives life but if improperly used takes physical life away. There is fire which is necessary for energy and living but also has an opposite effect. God let us know that if we put our hand in fire it will burn so listen carefully to His Will. It is God's Will that only goodness, love and serenity exist in our life, but we created adversity. It is now time for the soul to regain paradise and serenity. We are created to live in the Spirit of God. This is a place of sacred and Holy Peace. It is anything and everything that we desire.

We experience emotions, feelings and wonder related to this life. This is a journey with the purpose of learning to be in control of our will in order to do the will of God. Meditative prayer is a way to awareness of our Divine nature and spiritual inheritance. Each person has a natural desire to return home to paradise and serenity. Healing of the soul occurs when we learn that the one way home is the way of Love. Peace and serenity is the result as we respond to the genuine affection received in communion with God and all of creation.

All are of one family created by one God. A meeting of our mind and soul with another, is a union of individuals who are a unified creation in the Holy Spirit of the Creator. In God's desire for companionship, extension of the Divine Being and Creator took place. A connection or deep bond becomes apparent as we realize that all are sisters and brothers. Once recognition has transpired, our journey home begins. In this place, all again become one with infinite love and yet retain personal individuality. This is a spiritual alliance, a spiritual love.

All are divine beings formed in the image of God. Each person has the power to choose think and direct according to individual desire. All are part of the one God, one Spirit, and one Creator. We are a part of divinity incarnated in humanity. This is a learning experience in the purpose of living. Life is an individual journey for each person. A personal mission is becoming apparent as we continue on this path. The path of goodness and love is the way to follow. All creation is part of one Holy and eternal Spirit of God. We are living in the dawn of increasing consciousness that is revealing the reality of our united existence. Logic tells us that something is true and sensible, but it becomes part of our actual awareness when we sense it from within our mind and soul.

During prayer and sanctified meditation, all existence is observed as one and yet we maintain individuality. This leads to a place of peace and serenity. Focus on the Holy Spirit of God is an awakening that gives peace and meaning to life. In this communion of spirit, all are one in love. We reach this union, in the silence of the mind that is enlightening the entryway to the Light of God. We accomplish this connection between mind, body and soul through the creative power of God during meditative prayer which leads to serenity.

Sacred Serenity

As you pray, envision the sun reflecting on a stream of clear sparkling water. A field of gleaming particles surrounds the mountains in the distance. The air is warm and fresh. With each breath, become more peaceful and tranquil. The Light of God is surrounding and protecting you. There is a sense of total relaxation. Image yourself, resting beside a flowing stream. The flowing water is soothing as you listen to the sound of the moving waters over the glistening rocks and pebbles on the surface of the stream.

The sounds of nature and the birds singing create an atmosphere of delightful beauty. You hear soft music in the distance. The warmth of the sun combined with a gentle breeze causes a soothing effect on each part of your body. All your muscles begin to relax and a pleasant sense of peace fills your entire being. There is total silence as you wait for guidance. You receive inner guidance as you experience a feeling of Divine Love. All that occurs is in God's perfect way. A field of light energy surrounds you. This light appears as a transparent reflection, which absorbs only goodness. You are filled and surrounded by the Holy Light of God.

Imagine yourself moving into the water and feel the sensation of cool moving water as it causes an increased sense of calmness. Glide effortlessly over the stream and move toward the other side. Become aware of Sacred Light filling your body, mind, spirit and soul. Now you sense a feeling of oneness in spirit with nature and all living things as you continue to venture further inward within your mind. Within the silence, accept the mental images that are leading to unity, peace and happiness. You are at peace as you gaze into the crystal, clear waters. You feel the presence of the loving Light of God filling each particle of your being with a sensation of warmth and devotion.

It is as though the atmosphere surrounding your presence is a living force, communicating a feeling of serenity. You are aware of a feeling of togetherness, as you imagine the parts of an unfolding flower and understand that all unite in a magnificent and beautiful creation. Now as souls unify, a new phase of life begins with a bond of devotion and caring. As you join in a field of infinite love, you begin to become aware of the light that follows understanding. Your hope of fulfillment begins to become a reality.

This union in spirit reveals that to love one, it must be unconditional and include compassion and understanding for all. Only good exists. You ascend above all as you project joy, peace and universal unconditional love. Only good is created by love that is true. You are feeling peaceful, content, filled with the power of God's Love and the understanding that all are one in love. This is a place of Sacred Serenity leading to paradise. (3)

31. Living in the Moment with God

For one moment, quiet your mind and remain silent. All that exists is now. Just be there in the Holy Presence of God. The past, present, and future are one moment in the presence of time. As long as we remain in this place, there is peace. It is impossible to worry about the future or the past during this time of sacred stillness of the mind.

In this life, objects and people change in appearance but remain as the same original entity. We are living within the Holy Spirit of God in this everlasting moment. During a church service, I experienced a beautiful vision within my mind. It began with peaceful meditation and quietly listening to sacred music. I felt a sense divine quiet and inner peace. Just as the meditation was about to end, I envision a transformed scene which appeared to be out in nature. There was a glistening stream of water at the altar and across the stream, there was a man in a white gown who appeared as Jesus. He was joyful and smiling and gestured, communicating within my mind to be happy and joyful. I looked toward Him wondering why I was to be happy when I noticed that He was holding something in His arms. There was a beautiful purple pastor's prayer shawl visible in His Hands. I envisioned walking closer so that I could see what He was holding and saw that in His arms was a beautiful smiling baby. I thought, why, would He show me this beautiful child. I then realized that this child is going to move on to great service to God and mankind. Life is eternal, what appears as death is transition. Grief is the result because our beloved family member or friend is separated from us but truly, remains a memory, and in the reality of the present moment. In God's reality all exist within this moment.

How do we find the way to awareness of the presence of time? Follow the way of your heart. Trust and believe that God is caring for each of us now and always. Life exists in the present moment of all eternity. All that is seen, is now. All that we feel is with peace in knowing that all is well right now. We reach home through the heart of love and awareness of God's eternal loving presence. Moving inward in a state of Meditative Prayer is a method of accomplishing this. Move closer to the Light of God and all prevailing knowledge and awareness. With the power of the Holy Spirit of God, explore the precise environment of an inner universe and an outer never-ending existence. Move with your mind into the intricacy of a flower and travel through the hidden composition of all things.

We feel with others in a bond of affection due to the eternal presence of abiding Love and compassion that flows from God's Holy Spirit. The feeling of love, the feeling of kindness, the feeling of concern for another is an expression of our presence together with God who is always present, not as a distant being but as a kind and caring friend. Direct and express only goodness. All are forever one in the presence of time. Remain in this place, this moment, always realizing that all other thought is in the realm of expectation. This is a sacred place of order and harmony. It is where reconciliation transpires. Live in the presence of time where you are truly living in the Spirit of God. Remain focused on the presence of God and a vision of blessed eternity.

Abide in Love the Sacred Presence of God

In the Moment with God

Rest now in a comfortable position and imagine yourself in a beautiful place of silence, peace and serenity. Let your mind drift peacefully as you pray for guidance. Your mind is focused only on God's Holy Spirit. Envision a glistening stream of crystal, clear water. This is the stream of life. There is a flow into the past and a flow toward the future in the eternal Sacred Presence where all exists.

You are resting in a place of sanctified peace and silence. Wherever you journey along this stream of life, it is the here and now. If you move forward, it is your present moment and if you move backward, it is your present moment. Awareness of God's Holy Light leads you to a place of perfection that is present now and forever. Wherever you are, it is your present moment. The past is a memory and the future is an expectation. You may move toward the past and you may move toward the future but as it is experienced, it is existing now.

As you drift in this place, the sound of the moving stream becomes increasingly clear and soothing. The birds singing in the background create an atmosphere of soothing relaxation. The tranquil gentle movement of the water as you float peacefully fills your heart and mind with a feeling of total surrender to the natural flow of Holy Creation. You are guided enlightened and surrounded by the Holy Light of God. You may experience this moment with peace and trust that God's Divine Plan is working in a sacred and blessed way. Once you have learned to find this special place in the Presence of God, you will find it anywhere. You see beauty in all forms of life. Joy emanating from the mind of the Creator flows from your being. As you live in the Presence of the moment, you are living in the Spirit of God.

It is similar to awakening from a dream, where all was fragmented and vague, into actual conscious awareness. Meditative prayer extends your awareness creating a feeling of peace and sanctified healing. Your comprehension of the intricacies of creation begins to become vivid as though a clear light is improving your vision. This is the light of God. You are there instantaneously, in all that you do. Belief and trust that God is with you in the present moment and always leads to inner peace. Transformation in this present moment, in this life, occurs as you surrender to the Love, compassion and caring of God Who is forever present. The purpose of this meditative prayer is to bring out the good things that you find there and to share these things in an effort to help others in need. Most important, is to learn to find this place yourself. This is an inner experience that leads you to a vision of perfection as you live in the present reality with God. This is God's Reality.

32. Eternally in Remembrance

"But we all, with unveiled face, beholding as in a mirror the glory of the Lord, are being transformed into the same image from glory to glory, just as from the Lord, the Spirit." (2 Corinthians 3:18) (1)

Only the presence of God's Love will truly bring comfort during times of grief. It is inconceivable to think that God's beautiful children cease to exist. Even the concept of eternal life is difficult to understand. Our loved one is well, but we are living apart. In memory and in God's reality, all have new life that is eternal.

We are always together within the Love of God. Throughout life we gradually change in form, structure and mental ability. We acquire memories, develop a distinct personality, gain friends and develop attachments to family and loved ones. This person is now an individual entity who is forever part of sacred and divine memory and living in the presence of the eternal God.

Forever in Memory

"Therefore we do not lose heart, but though our outer man is decaying, yet our inner man is being renewed day by day. For momentary, light affliction is producing for us an eternal weight of glory far beyond all comparison, while we look not at the things which are seen, but at the things which are not seen; for the things which are seen are temporal, but the things which are not seen are eternal." (2 Corinthians 4:16-18) (1)

Birth into this life is as a pure and perfect infant. Love, care and nurturing helps to determine our outlook and motivation. As we grow and change, the infant is transformed and then exists only in memory.

Now there is a beautiful child who is loved and cared for. As a child, we continue to learn, grow, and change. This child is adored and cherished but is very soon transformed and exists only in memory.

We have grown to become an adolescent. There is the ability to recall our life experience in photos, events and knowledge. The new person is matured and changed. This process of growth continues, and soon the adolescent exists only in memory.

We continue to grown-up into an adult. The infant, child and adolescent exist only in memory, but we remain. The process of transforming growth continues and we exist as a newly evolved child of God, the entire self exists in the reality of this moment in time and eternally remains in memory.

Reality is living in the present. This belief promotes the concept of eternal life. That which exists now is everlasting. It is impossible for something to come from nothing. Life's substance, intelligence, mind and matter are timeless. This includes our individual personality as we grow to become one with God who perfectly preserves memory of all.

We are together forever in memory and in the present. Love and devotion bind one to the other. Our existence is timeless. Bonds of love form a link from one heart to the other. Movement out of the physical strengthens our spiritual relationship. Awareness that living is eternal will lighten your burden by revealing feelings hidden deep within your mind and transforming them through understanding and acceptance.

In an attempt to retain our connection with loved ones, there is a search for solutions. The inner mind understands clearly through renewal of thoughts that change feelings. Solutions involve looking for answers within our self that are received by the grace of God. It is clear as we contemplate the nature of life and understand that each person is precious and eternal. If the physical body suddenly vanished, the person would remain. The substance of living is eternal, our thoughts, feelings, and awareness of self continues without end. All are eternal children of God.

Move along the stream of time within yourself. The Spirit of God within us can change our feelings and renew faith. Belief in the eternal presence of those whom we love is a sacred gift of God. Within the infinite mind of God is memory of each soul. Memory is more than an intangible substance, it is the reality of an existing object or the self of one who has changed in appearance. Release beliefs that are causing any difficulty now, or allow them to move into your conscious mind and then deal with it in a manner that will lead to happiness and healing. You are an eternal, beautiful and perfect child of God.

We are surrounded and protected by the Light of God Who gives insight to understand that nothing is ever truly lost. With this knowledge, we are together forever in memory and in reality. Life is eternal we are always with those whom we love. People are transformed but never lost. This is our gift in the presence of the moment. We are together forever in the Love and Presence of God.

A Gift of Remembrance

Now pray for guidance that the Holy Spirit of God will lead you into the stream of eternal living and Sacred Spiritual communication. Ask for wisdom and understanding; this is a special and Holy Gift. Rest each part of your body, from the top of your head to the bottom of your feet. Feel a wave of relaxation through your body as a peaceful sensation becomes apparent.

Only that which is of God can influence you in any way. Imagine yourself resting in a beautiful location of peace and comfort. You are completely safe and secure. All that you need for comfort is available for you. In this protected environment, you are going to image yourself moving along a passageway to a place of enlightenment. Envision a soothing movement leading to your destination.

Memory is stored in a safe place within your mind and the sacred Mind of God for retrieval as needed. Your direction is now toward the future. Existence is timeless in this state of being. You are at peace in a safe and holy place. There is a feeling of security and love. Your mind is free of concern. Feel a sense of union with all creation. You are now resting, feeling tired and beginning to relax completely. You are safe and secure; only good can influence you in any way. Image yourself surrounded and protected by God's holy and shielding light. Request divine guidance as you continue on this journey.

The stream is leading toward a light in the distance. It is clear and bright. It is leading the way toward your destination. As the light moves toward you there is a sense of peace. The movement of the light creates a sensation of peace. There is expectation of a new and special event. You remain completely secure. It is comforting and safe. There is a feeling of love in an affectionate environment. Sense the warmth and contentment. You are peaceful and secure as you feel the presence of those whom you love. Be there for a moment and communicate with your loved ones within the Holy Spirit of God.

As you look up, there is a spark of light in the distance, revealing a new and fulfilling way of life. Within the silence of your inner, mind you can move forward in time, back in time or remain in the present moment. You accomplish this through the grace of God. As you rest there become aware of any time or place that will reveal your present mission and purpose. Learn from this experience. You are an eternal and beautiful person. Life is a continual cycle of renewal. This is growth that brings you closer to your highest ideal and the fulfillment of your purpose in the scheme of existence. Take a moment to reflect on this sacred purpose as you live eternally in the Holy Spirit of God. Bring into the present all the knowledge and insight that you require for purposeful living and awareness that you possess the gift of presence in the moment with God.

33. Creative Light of God

Good thought leads to good feelings and a vision of the Light of God in all creation. Holy Light, leading to peace, is created in life through the transformation of the mind and soul. The human concept of reality is the result of information received throughout life. Meditative Prayer and imagery opens a door that allows light to enter giving clear vision of God's reality. We can visualize the Light of God in all Creation within our mind. Beliefs based on love bring about a peaceful mind. Meditating on the Light and Love of God is similar to implanting a trustworthy directive for peace into the mind. The Light of God, that is visible in all creation, is a gateway to Heaven on Earth.

There are many different beliefs but only One God and many manifestations of the One God who knows all people, speaks all languages and loves all unconditionally. God reveals the eternal self as, Father, Mother, Sister, Brother, Friend, Teacher, Doctor, Nurse, Healer, in every vocation, act of love, help and caring. We see God in the face of every person. God is heard and felt in the wind, rain, snow and all the elements of the earth. God is seen in the Sun, Moon, Stars and all of nature. God is everywhere and in everything. Throughout the ages, God preached through the prophets, the saints, spiritual and religious leaders and God Speaks to us every day in our mind, heart and soul. We only must listen. We are blessed with guiding Angels and Holy inspiration in which God Speaks directly to our mind and heart as we pray and meditate. I thank you God for these blessings.

The Human Body is a miraculous creation. The inner mind believes all that it encounters as reality even if it is imagined. Clear mental visualization will cause a thought to be accepted by the mind as reality. Images that are transmitted to the subconscious mind are very important in life. They influence the mental, emotional and physical self. These impressions are stored in the inner mind, and to some extent conscious awareness. Whatever the mind receives is what it creates. Through a series of actions or events, the mind will create the conditions of a belief. Just as an athlete uses mental rehearsal, you have the ability to create Light in God's Creation within your mind by accepting only thoughts and ideas that are in harmony with God's reality of truth and goodness. This a way of living in the Spirit of God.

Renewal of our life occurs as we quiet our mind to receive guidance and then use that guidance to image God's perfect reality. Create a clear image within the mind. We have the power to change the effect of any condition in our life. See, feel and hear only the good that exists in all people and all situations. Renewal then occurs in a manner that is right and perfect. By the Grace of God, we are the master and creator of our life. We are given free will with the intension of using it in a way that will lead to completion of our mission and then move on to a greater phase of existence in the Light of God's Creation.

Renewal of Spirit in the Light of God

Rest in a comfortable position and pray for Holy Guidance. Let your eyes close naturally. Become aware of your surroundings as your eyes close. Image within your mind, your self-surrounded and protected by a shield Holy God Light. This light is reflecting like a mirror within your mind. Image yourself surrounded and protected by God's divine light. Quiet your mind and ask for guidance. Only good can influence you in any way.

Imagine walking along a beautiful lake enjoying the beauty of nature. Bend forward toward the water and observe closely. Touch the water. It feels soothing and pleasantly warm. You sense that these are healing waters. Just continue to touch it with your hand and feel the healing Light of God entering your total being. Become aware of a rainbow aura surrounding your body and merging with each cell, there is unity in the silence of the Holy Light of God that is seen in all of creation.

The Light of God is reflecting on the surface of the lake. The water is sparkling clear and glistening with the rays of the sun. You feel a wave of tranquility flowing around and through your body causing you to become more peaceful and at ease. You are completely safe and protected as you continue on your journey. Only good can influence you in any way. There is a sense of inspirational messages flowing into your mind.

As you gaze at the sparkling water, there is a reflection from within you that is important in helping you to receive Holy inspiration. You are one with the light and in unity with the Creative Spirit of God. God's Holy Light is within you and extending into the surrounding area. Now as you look forward the Light of God's Creation is radiant and clear. There are mountains in the distance and a waterfall leading into a stream of running water. The sun shining on the water is sparkling. The movement gives an effect of small bubbling diamonds twirling on the water. A cool breeze is causing a movement in the surrounding trees, grass and wild flowers that give an impression of living nature.

As you begin to gain insight into the Light of God's Creation, a gradual awakening is in progress. You perceive the world through your sacred and holy senses. With the Light of God, impressions within your mind are a perfect renewal of belief systems. Your inner mind, filled with the Light of God, knows exactly what to do, so just rest there and accept infinite and holy guidance. Your connection with God's divine mind is working out a perfect solution leading to absolute renewal. The Light of God's creation is clear and enlightening your life.

34. The Flow and Breath of Life

"Everyone who drinks of this water will thirst again; but whoever drinks of the water that I will give him shall never thirst; but the water that I will give him will become in him a well of water springing up to eternal life."(John 4:13-15) (1)

The flow and breath of life is the progression of the soul along the span of eternal life. Just as the memory of self as an infant and a child are part of the continuum of living, memory of all that we are becomes part of the extended self that is everlasting. Self-awareness and acceptance of our Divine nature are the beginning of realization that we are an eternal, perfect and beautiful child of God.

It is in love, acceptance, forgiveness, and learning to live in the Holy Spirit of God that mending and healing occurs. A quiet mind creates an image of clarity and wellness. We reach a level of highly evolved consciousness that is one with God. Awareness of our connection with God clears the path for a Holy mission to be fulfilled. Loving warmth between people is transcendent. Those in need require the love support and care of another person. The flow and breath of life leads to sanctification of the soul and loving interaction that is eternal.

The satisfaction in knowing that a task is completed leads to a higher level of functioning in the Spirit of Holiness. This is our purpose in the process of living. As a Faith Community Nurse, I was recently called to visit a patient in the hospital. I received a message on my cell phone to please visit someone. It was not the usual day that I do pastoral care visitation but I thought that it may be an emergency so I immediately went to the hospital. This is a young and lovely woman who had a terminal illness. My visit was unexpected. I explained that I received a call from the church to visit and that I do visitation through the hospital chaplain's office. She said I am not religious, I don't go to church. I was previously told that she is agnostic. I explained that a hospital chaplain is non-denominational and that visits are for any type of support that may be needed.

As I looked at her, I and saw a young and beautiful child of God. She is radiant with a spirit of love and kindness. Even during this serious illness her voice was sweet and loving. It only took a moment to feel the Love in her heart and understand that God is Love. The word of God is written within our mind, heart and soul. God is living where there is Love. This is confirmed by all who spoke of her. She is filled with love, kindness, caring and compassion. The Love that filled her heart never dies, it is the flow and breathe of all life. Her soul is living in the Spirit of God's unconditional Love and in the mind and heart of those who love her. This is a place of God's reality, she is living in the Spirit of God's Peace.

A life filled with empathy, compassion, understanding, forgiveness and caring is reaching the deepest level of bonding in God's Love. The most important of all is love. We are filled with the Spirit of God when we consciously and with all our mind, soul and spirit make a decision to unconditionally give and accept love. It is the way to finding the Spirit of God because God is Love. Only good can exist where there is sacred love. Heaven is anything and everything that we want. This includes all the joy that is experienced here and now.

The flow and breath of life moves effortlessly as we trust in the Love of

God. Drift by each difficulty with confidence and courage. Experience the beauty of nature and all things. The air is fresh and clear and there a sense of unity with God in this realm of inner peace. We are eternal children of God who are gifted with the ability to live in harmony with all and be a true help and blessing to others.

Breath of Life for Healing

Breathe in deeply and exhale slowly as you rest and pray. There is an awareness of existence in the spiritual and mental dimension of life. You are comfortable and rest in the knowledge that all is well. You are guided and protected by God's Holy Spirit. Imagine yourself sitting comfortably in a beautiful garden. This is your garden. This is your home in the in the Spirit of God. You have the ability to visualize and create it in a manner that is perfect for you and as it is God's perfect will. The concerns of the day are a vague memory as you relax by a peaceful stream.

The sun is setting and reflecting a vibrant illumination of colors upon the sky; this light is brightening the atmosphere and creating the sensation of sacred holiness. You are feeling a sense of contentment in the presence of God's Holy Spirit. Your focus is on the present, and the experience of inner elation derived from being at home with all whom you care for. You are at home with your spiritual family in the Love of God.

The flow and breath of life is now becoming clear. You are beginning to flow peacefully along the course of living. Holy inspiration is a sacred breath of life. This is a major accomplishment and now you are ready to move forward with love and confidence in knowing that you have the ability to return to your place of love and peace.

During Meditative Prayer, view life from a distance and see a complete picture according to the Holy will of God. This reveals a course of living where there is a natural flow of life. All have a purpose and a plan. You choose your plan in this stream of living and it is your responsibility to ensure that it flows gracefully. Your inner experience of that place of reconciliation is a reality within your mind. All are one and united in a bond of humanity. Deeper thought reveals that all substance is composed of the same material; it is only the rate of vibration that give objects a solid appearance. You are living in the Spirit of God.

Clear your mind of all thought and let yourself, be guided by the Holy Spirit. As you meditate, receive answers to your prayers. Receive Divine guidance from within. You are ascending closer to the spiritual realm of understanding and enlightenment. Guidance flows from a place of goodness and perfection. Your consciousness is elevated toward an ascended vision of reality. There is eternal and perfect clarity of purpose. Quiet your mind and listen quietly for answers. Your conscious mind is passive and clear. Only good can influence you in any way. You are existing in the reality of God. You are living in the Holy Spirit of God. You are in total control and receptive to Holy and divine intervention.

An elevated state of consciousness is one in which you know and understand yourself and your relationship to all. You are a channel, of love, a channel of healing, and a channel of peace. Extend this image with clarity of purpose. Rest there in the Spirit of God. When you are ready return feeling wonderful in every way and bring the guidance, you receive with you. You are a blessing to others by the grace of God. You are living in the Spirit of God. You are receiving God's Breath of Life for Inner Healing.

35. Home Living in the Spirit of God

There is wonder beyond imagination as we envision and become aware of all the natural beauty that God created. We are eternally living in the Spirit of God's Peace. It is a place of Love within our mind and Heart. It is found with the power of the Holy Spirit and the Love of God within. Trust, faith and belief is all that is required. That which our mind believes is reality. By the Grace, and as a gift, of God, we are the creator of our personal reality, health and feelings, because all are one within the Holy Spirit.

During meditative prayer, the imagination which is leading to a place of silence and peace, is the gateway to Living in the Spirit of God. By the grace of God, we enlighten the path toward inner vision where awareness increases and reveals an image of God. It is almost equivalent to attempting to describe sacred music filling the air on a peaceful brilliant day. Words are not sufficient to grace the gentle warmth of a loving feeling that was once dormant but now, is flowing like a current of pure water. Abide in Love and visualize, living in the Presence of God. This vision transforms into reality as we continue on this journey. This is a real and beautiful place created by the power of God's Pure Love.

What and where is this real and beautiful place. The universe is defined as "all existing matter and space considered as a whole; the cosmos. The universe is believed to be at least 10 billion light years in diameter and contains a vast number of galaxies; it has been expanding since its creation in the Big Bang about 13 billion years ago." (www.merriam-webster.com/dictionary/universe) This definition states that the universe was created and that it is expanding. This is the time of the creation of the universe, according to the book of Genesis.

"In the beginning God created the heavens and the earth. The earth was formless and void, and darkness was over the surface of the deep, and the Spirit of God was moving over the surface of the waters. Then God said, "Let there be light"; and there was light. God saw that the light was good; and God separated the light from the darkness. God called the light day, and the darkness He called night. And there was evening and there was morning, one day." (1) (Genesis 1: 1-6)

According to Quantum theory of *imaginary time* which is an authentic scientific concept. Ordinary or real, time is a horizontal line. On the left is the past, and on the right is the future. But there's another kind of time in the vertical direction. This is what is called imaginary time. It is not the kind of time we normally encounter. But scientifically it is just as real, as real time. It runs in a direction different from the type of time we experience. Imaginary time is a way of looking at the time dimension as if it were a dimension of space: you can move forward and backward along imaginary time, just like you can move right and left in space. The universe has not existed forever but the creator of the universe is eternal.

My knowledge of science is very basic and I am far from qualified to give scientific explanations but I have a sincere interest and respect for all that God created including science. God is all the building blocks of the universe because all was created by God from nothing but the substance of self. As stated, divine mind, matter, intelligence, feeling, creative energy and great love withdrew into its Self and then extended Its Self, and is continuing to expand.

During Meditative Prayer, imagination leads you to enter a dimension of consciousness in which you are existing in a spiritual reality. Paradise is a place in the mind and an actual reality. As we change our mind, there is an actual change in the real world. This is a place of the evolved soul. We come to believe that God's kingdom is universal and on earth as it is in heaven. In the beginning, we separated from this place of origin. *(1)* *(Genesis 1: 26:28) "Then God said, "Let Us make man in Our image, according to Our likeness; and let them rule over the fish of the sea and over the birds of the sky and over the cattle and over all the earth, and over every creeping thing that creeps on the earth." God created man in His own image, in the image of God He created him; male and female He created them. God blessed them."*

It is a long journey. Our mission to return to God has followed a pathway leading to a perfect place of peace. As our consciousness evolves, awareness of this sacred identity becomes evident. See, feel, listen and believe in this good and loving creation of God and that we are living in God's reality. This is a natural world of peacefulness and harmony. Accept this gift and use it in a manner that will benefit all. Our most vivid dreams transform into a reality of peace and joy. We have faith and confidence in the Spirit of God with us now and eternally.

Finding Our Heavenly Home

Rest now, pray and ask for guidance from God's Holy Spirit. Focus on the Spirit of God leading you to a place where your mind is at peace, clear of all thought, and receptive to the Holy Will of God. Sacred and distinct inner vision within God's reality will guide your way. Take a deep breath now. Breathe out slowly, take another deep breath and exhale slowly. Begin to feel rested now, calm, and content. Your mind is becoming more receptive to inner Holy Guidance. This will cause a deep and lasting sense of peace that will remain for as long as required, in God's perfect way.

You are moving into a deep peaceful state of relaxation. Drift and rest now, free of any distraction, and allow yourself to enjoy this very peaceful state of being. Your conscious mind can relax completely. Your inner mind will receive and understand. Now visualize within your mind that the Spirit of God is there with you to assist and guide. Envision yourself going to God and inviting God to be with you. Together, you are now going to open a door within the mind. Trust, believe and have faith as you journey toward this doorway leading to inner knowledge and understanding. This is a place of learning.

Now imagine sitting comfortably in a perfect and beautiful location. It is a lovely, mild, day. There is a soothing warm breeze. The air is brilliant and refreshing. Feel yourself moving into this place, that you are visualizing within your mind. It will come to the light within your mind automatically. A feeling of Divine peace touches the atmosphere with an aura of boundless serenity. There is consciousness of wellbeing as you view in the distance a path lead you toward your heavenly home and living in the spirit of God. Walk together toward the path.

The day is clear and warm. The air is fresh. Take a deep breath, and begin to walk slowly upward. The path is direct and flowing like as stream of air. Become more peaceful and relaxed with each step. Receive guidance that is Holy and Sacred as you continue. You are completely safe and secure in the Hands of God. Only good and loving sensation or ideas will influence you in any way.

Move upward, reaching higher levels of awareness. Your inner mind understands that any impression within your mind that has been causing a problem is now being resolved naturally and automatically. This pleasant experience is revising any beliefs within your mind that have been causing a problem or misunderstanding. You know that you are safe, secure and protected by God's divine presence.

Focus now on the presence and love of God. Extend your hand and repeat I want to be in Your Holy presence eternally as I journey toward my home. I pray Dear God that you take my hand and lead me to living in your Holy Presence. Teach me to truly love and to truly care. I pray for forgiveness and guidance. Fill me with your Spirit of Love, Peace and Compassion for all people. I ask this sincerely.

The birds are singing and a gentle breeze is rustling through the trees. Sit and rest. It is so soothing and peaceful to drift into a deep peaceful state of relaxation. Realize that all of nature is perfect. The trees, flowers, animals, birds are in such perfect form. All natural things are functioning in exquisite order. We can project into the essence of a leaf or a flower and realize its intricate beauty and perfection.

Natural things are a perfect, flawless creation of God. The animals, the birds, fish in the stream, all know exactly what to do, in order to remain perfect and healthy. It is within their nature to know. God created us to know. Just as we naturally to know how to rest and relax when needed. All of nature is automatically aware of that which is appropriate, when to rest and sleep, and what activity we need for health and peace. The important knowledge that we are receiving is that living in a beautiful reality is a natural process. All things are a perfect creation. There is a Holy purpose in the design of all things. Each vision of beauty is individual. Image your perfect reality within your mind and a picture is created that will manifest outwardly.

Now feel the peace and contentment. There is a sense of peace and relaxation as you observe the beauty of nature, listen to the sounds, and feel the splendor of these surroundings. Our mission and method of accomplishment becomes apparent because we see it everywhere and in everything. We are home now, creating within the mind a vision of our perfect home where we are living in the spirit of God. See it clearly and view each detail. Believe what we are seeing, hearing, and feeling within the mind and soul. With this vision see that we are living in perfect peace and filled with the Holy Love of God. Only good beliefs or feelings can be of any influence. A shield of God's Sacred light surrounds and protects.

Know that God is a part of all as we create our reality according to God's Holy Will. Rest and continue visualizing your perfect reality. The Holy Spirit of God is automatically working out solutions according to God's Holy and Sacred plan for living. This will lead to our special place and spiritual home in the Spirit of God. In this place, there is love, peace and contentment. God's Love fills us with a feeling of kindness, empathy, and compassion. We fill our home with goodness and envision it absorbed into the mind and heart of all. Prayer, meditation, loving kindness, empathy and compassion are a few of the keys to the door of our heavenly home. Open each door and enter. We envisioned the path and now we know the way to living in the spirit of God.

36. Living in the Spirit of God's Peace

"Blessed are the Peacemakers for they will be called children of God." (Matthew 5:9) (1)

In a dream, two friends, a male and a female, were lost. They suddenly disappeared. I was told the name of a state where they were seen and that I could communicate with them. I then, suddenly, heard their voice and I began to talk with them. It seemed like, I was talking with spiritual beings. I looked up at what appeared to be a large window and observed that they were standing on a lovely city street. I said that I was looking for them and asked, "Where are you"? They said that they were well and know where they are going; a place is reserved for them; it is called Omega 22. I awakened from the dream feeling relieved that I knew where they were going. I wondered where and what is Omega 22 so I searched for it on the internet. This is what I found. *"I am the Alpha and the Omega, the first and the last, the beginning and the end." "Blessed are those who wash their robes, so that they may have the right to the tree of life, and may enter by the gates into the city."*

(Revelation 22:13-14) (1)

"Now, little children, abide in Him, so that when He appears, we may have confidence and not shrink away from Him in shame at His coming. If you know that He is righteous, you know that everyone also who practices righteousness is born of Him." (1 John 2: 27-28) (1) God lives, all live in the Spirit of God. The Human Being is a temple of the Holy Spirit. Care for this Holy Temple with love, and receive Sacred Blessings. Extend Love to all creation, and Love your Self. The children of God inherit this Earth which is created as a paradise; it is a beautiful Garden with flowers and trees of every kind and fruit to eat. All human desire is fulfilled in God's heavenly garden but, our glory is temporally hidden. Freedom of will, with the human ability to contradict Divine Law, creates separation from the Holy Presence. Now is the moment for return to God through selflessness. We extend our self into oneness with the Divine Creator, and remain, as the genuine self who is a friend of God. Of our own free will, God's will be done.

"Then the Lord God said, "Behold, the man has become like one of Us, knowing good and evil; and now, he might stretch out his hand, and take also from the tree of life, and eat, and live forever" therefore the Lord God sent him out from the garden of Eden, to cultivate the ground from which he was taken. So He drove the man out; and at the east of the garden of Eden He stationed the cherubim and the flaming sword which turned every direction to guard the way to the tree of life." (1) (Genesis 3: 22-24)

A soul created to be free and a child of God, with all power and intelligence, entered into human bondage. All conscious knowledge of our origin is relinquished. We enter this world in a sense, without awareness of our genuine nature. Now we are increasing in awareness of our spiritual self. The first man and woman lost their place in paradise and all of mankind followed. There came into existence separation due to disobedience to God's Will. Now in the present moment and in the presence of God, the time is here for return. The purpose of humanity is to dwell in Heaven on Earth and abide in Love. Our mind and intelligence is expanding to a level of sacred consciousness.

Imagination and visualization is much more than a method of healing and mental relaxation. It is a guide for the human mind and soul. We are growing and evolving into a stage where the soul and spirit are free to transcend the physical at will. We naturally know, and understand the feelings of another. The human body is physical but possesses a spiritual nature. All are perfect and possess inner and outer beauty. We have the ability and power to create, image, and visualize an environment of peace and happiness according to the Holy Will of God. Love is a way of life, there is spiritual unity and loving connection with our spiritual family and all life. We have the ability to be together always, in a spiritual bond.

Thought creates reality by the grace of God. We use our free will to choose the good. Awareness of another way of living is always an option but intelligence and an elevated level of consciousness gives us the insight to know which to choose. We are kind and forgiving. The concept of adversity is non-existent due to our decision to accept only the good. Knowing the difference provides the insight needed to truly feel joy and happiness in our way of living.

We communicate with our mind and commune in spirit. We have access to other worlds and planets. There is the ability to travel through dimensions of consciousness. This is our present reality. The Earth is green and beautiful. It is a magnificent garden of loveliness beyond comprehension and filled with the Holy Spirit of God. This is our home and thought is all that is required to transport us there in the presence of time. Home is here, right where we are in this present moment. Just close, your eyes quiet your mind and become aware of Living in the Spirit of God's Peace. "Thy Will be done, on Earth as it is in Heaven" (The Lord's Prayer) Take our hand Dear God and lead us there. This is our mission. This is our vision. The loving hands of Angels embrace us as we are born in this place of healing and serenity.

Abide in Love, in the Spirit of a Loving God, where peace and love is the way of interacting and bonding with all people. A loving relationship builds an environment and atmosphere of magnificence beyond ordinary comprehension. Unity is love, kindness, compassion and caring. There is guidance for living in this place of healing and serenity as we quiet our mind and experience this place of love within our mind and heart in the Spirit of God.

Frances Stroh

Meditative Prayer for Peace

"Be perfected; be comforted; be of the same mind; live in peace: and the God of love and peace shall be with you." (2 Corinthians 13:11)

Dear God take our hand and lead us. Teach us to live in Peace and Abide in Love. Guide us to Sacred Presence according to Your Divine Will. Help us to overcome all obstacles; restore, and let there be, peace in our heart and on this Earth. Bring us close to your Spirit of Holiness. Surround and protect us with your Holy Spirit. We are of One Holy Origin. Show us the way to Your Love and Peace Dear Lord.

Quiet your mind and allow the Holy Spirit of Peace fill your heart with Abiding Love. Consider God's Holy and Deeper meaning. Allow God to enter our soul and help us to know that we are of one mind in a place where we live in Sacred Peace. Consider how the truth and power of the Word of God affects life and actions. Receive Holy Inspiration. Faith is the validation of the invisible, and the belief in its reality. Faith is recognizing as reality that which is unseen by the intellects physical senses. "That they would seek God, if perhaps they might grope for Him and find Him, though He is not far from each one of us; for in Him we live and move and exist, as even some of your own poets have said, 'For we also are His children.'"(Acts 17:27-2) "Now faith is the assurance of things hoped for, the conviction of things not seen." (Hebrews 11:1) (1) Abide in Love, the Sacred Presence of God, where we receive the Blessing of Inner Peace that is extended to all of Divine Creation.

Sacred Reading

Mankind learned the difference between good and evil. Now we may stretch out our hand toward the hand of God with the knowledge of God's eternal goodness and love; and live forever in the Spirit of God's Peace. The hand of God will lead us home through all obstacles. Be aware of only God's reality; in mind, heart, soul and spirit. Think only Sacred Good, see only Sacred Good, hear only Sacred Good and speak only Sacred Good. Abide in Love in the Sacred Presence of God.

"Come, you who are blessed of My Father, inherit the kingdom prepared for you from the foundation of the world. For I was hungry, and you gave Me something to eat; I was thirsty, and you gave Me something to drink;

Abide in Love the Sacred Presence of God

I was a stranger, and you invited Me in; naked, and you clothed Me; I was sick, and you visited Me; I was in prison, and you came to Me.' Then the righteous will answer Him, 'Lord, when did we see You hungry, and feed You, or thirsty, and give You something to drink? And when did we see you a Stranger, and invite you in, or naked, and clothe you? When did we see You Sick, or in prison, and come to visit you? The King will answer and say to them, 'Truly I say to you, to the extent that you did it to one of these Brothers of Mine, even the least of them, you did it to Me.' (1) (Matthew 25: 34-40

Fill us with your Holy Spirit of Love. "So, as those who have been chosen of God, holy and beloved, put on a heart of compassion, kindness, humility, gentleness and patience;" (1) Colossians 3:12 Promote Love, caring, and peace between individuals, families and in all the world. Love one another, we are one. I am the Lord your God who is one and part of all. The name of God is Sacred, Love one another. Love all people and all nations.

Bring us to a place of rest and peace. Teach us trust and have faith that dissolves the worries of this world. God rested but creation continues to expand and extend to all in the Spirit of Love. Keep every day Holy. Rest mind, body and soul with the knowledge that God knows all our needs. Let there be Light, and peace. Honor all people with Love and respect. All are One Holy and united family. This includes all of the universe.

Help us to Care for and love all people, nations and life. Love the Earth and all its' creatures. All that exists is here for us. Love and share always knowing the great blessing that giving to one is a gift to God and to all. These gifts are eternal and as we give we receive. Be faithful to God, to our spiritual family, and the complete and true self. Trust and have faith that all will be done according to perfect and Sacred Divine Will.

Help us to see the whole truth. See a reflection of self in all people. Understand the needs and feelings of all forms in creation. Respect each person and creature that inhabits this earth and throughout this universe. Everything is our eternal inheritance and everything is God and is God's. It is blessed to give. Teach us to Meditate in our heart be still and know God.

Frances Stroh

Abide in Love the Spirit of God's Peace

"No one has seen God at any time; if we love one another, God abides in us, and His love is perfected in us." (1 John 4:12) (1) We love and live in the Spirit of God.

Rest your mind body and soul in the Holy presence of God knowing that God is Love. Pray and ask that God's Holy Spirit be with you to guide, protect and enlighten the path. Envision within your mind being together with all who you love. With hands joined in a bond of loving affection, we will cross the stream toward our home and unity in the in the Spirit of God. Move into the water of the silent stream and feel the touch of life, the energy of love that flows from God's Holy Spirit. It is warm and soothing. Our peace is total and complete. Sacred and holy love is flowing to fill our life.

Now as we reach the other side move out of the water and walk toward a gate. The path is lined with glorious flowers of multiple vivid colors. The air is clear. The day is brilliant. We feel peaceful and loving as we move through the door where all are one in God's Loving Spirit. God's Light enters and the light flows from one to the other. The intensity of light is brilliant as a golden aura. There is now a movement and connection as we become of one mind within the mind of God's Holy Spirit of God. The flow of Light continues to move toward our heart. In this loving silence, all is still; all is Love, as we continue toward Living in the Spirit of God. As souls commune in spirit, sacred Light is shining into an eternal vision of beauty and clarity, luminous in color, overwhelming in feeling with knowledge of our self in an atmosphere of loving spirit.

As we reach out in a gesture of loving affection, the light of that love flows like a stream turning darkness into light. A door to the inner mind opens giving a sense of inner vision. The purpose of this awakening is to extend this Light and Love in assistance to all that need it. This journey leads to a very simple path. It is the way of Love that leads to peace. We learn something very basic and yet more difficult than imagined and that is to Love entirely with mind, heart and soul. A communion in spirit enlightens the way. We are one in loving dedication. Comprehending this love for another requires learning to care for the self. The self is extending in order to be as one with all. When I understand what I feel then I can relate to another and have true empathy. When I know, what I need then I understand what you need. As I care about myself, I care about you. You are "My Love" in the Stream Of Love where all are one and Living in the Spirit of God.

Once this connection is complete, we are united. The bond remains as we work together *in spirit. It is in performing a purposeful function, with concern and genuine caring, that love is complete. Its purpose is to generate a flow of God's Holy Spirit, from one to another into an atmosphere of peace and love. This may act as a flash of God's Holy Light, kindling a warm glow, in the heart of others. As the stream of love flows and merges, we extend love, devotion, and peace. Hands reach out, and we know that this is Home in the Spirit of God where all unite, never again to part. Bring this vision of Gods' Holy Love with you as you live in the Spirit of God's Peace. "Then he showed me a river of the water of life, clear as crystal, coming from the throne of God and of the Lamb, in the middle of its street. On either side of the river was the tree of life, bearing twelve kinds of fruit, yielding its fruit every month; and the leaves of the tree were for the healing of the nations." (Revelation 22:1-2) (1)*

Awaken now and see the way to a Blessed and Holy Reality. We are sleeping and living in a dream. Awaken now and the Divine Light will glow in our mind, heart and soul to enlighten our life and thoughts. This is a way of Living in the Spirit of God's Peace. "And this commandment we have from Him, that the one who loves God should love his brother also." God Is Love. (1 John 4:21) (1)

"Surely goodness and mercy shall follow me all the days of my life and I shall dwell in the house of the Lord forever." (Psalm 23:6) (1) Abide in Love and we live in the Spirit of God's Peace. Abide in Love, the Sacred Presence of God.

http://www.franstroh.com/

http://www.tolcare.com/

About the Author

Frances Stroh RN, MA, FCN, is a Registered Nurse with experience in Mental Health, Psychiatry, School Nursing, and Holistic Nursing. She is presently a Faith Community Nurse, mother of two children and grandmother of eight of God's beautiful children.

Frances Graduated from Queensborough Community College with a degree in Nursing Science. She then continued her education in the areas of Community Health, Counseling Psychology, Holistic Nursing, and Faith Community/Parish Nursing. She attended State University of New York in Old Westbury and Saint John's University of Practical Theology LA. And received a Master of Arts Degree in Counseling Psychology with honors, Magna Cum Laude.

Memberships include, the American Holistic Nurses Association, American Psychiatric Nurses Association, Nurse Healers Professional Association, NGH, Health Ministries Association (HHA), The International Parish Nurse Resource Center and Evangelical Lutheran Parish Nurse Association.

Employment included positions as staff nurse and nurse management at City Hospital Center Elmhurst, New York; South Nassau Community Hospital, Oceanside New York; Nassau Center for Developmentally Disabled, Syosset New York; Nassau University Medical Center, East Meadow, New York; and Hempstead Public Schools where she was School Nurse at Hempstead High School for eleven years. She taught CPR and First Aid for the American Heart Association and the American Red Cross for more than 20 years. As a Holistic Nurse she practiced as an independent provider; teaching and implementing Stress Management; including Biofeedback and mind/body self-regulation techniques, self-hypnosis, imagery, and meditation.

Since 2009, Frances is a Parish Nurse at Our Savior Lutheran Church in Vero Beach Florida. She is a Eucharistic Minister for homebound and hospital patients, leader of Sisters in Christ Care and Prayer and Meditation Group. Assisted in Health Screenings, Bible Camp for Children, Blood Pressure Screening, Health Assessment, Healing Services, and administrative activities. She is active in Church activities including Bible Study and God Pause (Lectio Davina). Frances is also a Pastoral Care volunteer at Indian

River Medical Center in Vero Beach. She assists in the Chaplin's office and does patient visitation, and is one of the leaders in a Spirituality Group at the IRMC Behavioral Health Center in Vero Beach.

Writing includes meditative imagery for health and inner healing, behavior modification and managing individual client problems. She is the author of the book "Valley of the Silent Stream, Meditative Imagery for Inner Healing", "Awakening to the Holy Light of Christ, Touch of Life Meditative Prayer for Inner Peace" and she is one of the authors of the book God's Work Our Hands, Tools for Health Ministry; A foundation for Building a Health Ministry/Parish Nurse Program. This was written and organized with a group of nurses from ELCA (Evangelical Lutheran Church America Parish Nurse Association. Awakening to the Holy Light of Christ, is a Guide to the Art of Silence and Christian Meditation; inspired during Prayer and Meditation at Our Savior.

Recently, Frances was a presenter at Joining the Song of Faith Community Nursing Westberg Symposium 2015 at the Peabody Memphis Hotel. She and two parish nurses from Our Savior Lutheran Church Vero Beach, FL presented "Meditative Prayer for Spiritual Care." Which is based upon her current book "Abide in Love the Sacred Presence of God, Meditative Prayer for Spiritual Care." The entire presentation is posted on the website http://www.franstroh.com

Reference/Related Readings

1. New American Standard Bible, the Lockman Foundation, 1960,1962,1963,1968,1971,1972,1973,1975,1977,1995,

2. Catechism of the Catholic Church, New York London Toronto Sydney Auckland: Image Doubleday, 1994

3. Valley of the Silent Stream Touch of Life Meditative Imagery for Inner Healing by Frances Stroh RN, MA, Bloomington, Indiana: Author House, 2006.

4. Awakening to the Holy Light of Christ, Touch of Life Meditative Prayer for Inner Peace, Frances Stroh RN, MA, FCN, 2014

5. Faith Community Nursing Scope and Standards of Practice, American Nurses Association and Health Ministries Association, 2005

6. Holistic Nursing, a Handbook for Practice by Barbara Montgomery Dossey, Lynn Keegan, Cathie E Gazette, American Holistic Nurses Association, 1999

7. The Healing Presence, Spiritual Exercises for Healing, Wellness and Recovery by Dr. Reverend Thomas A Droege, Youth and Family Institute, 1996,

8. Immortal Diamond, the Search for Our True Self by Richard Rohr, Jossey-Bass, 2013

9. The Holy Bible, Parallel Version, King James Version/New International version (NIV) 1985 Zonderan

10. Foundations for Centering Prayer and the Christian Contemplative Life by Thomas Keating Includes: Open Mind, Open Heart Invitation to Love, the Mystery of Christ, Blumsbury Publishing, Reprinted 2011

11. The Holy Bible, New International Version (NIV) 1988, Zondcran

12. The Other Side of Silence, a Guide to Christian Meditation by Thomas T Kelsey, Paulist Press, NY, Toronto, 1976

13. Sanctuary of the Soul, Journey into Meditative Prayer by Richard J. Foster, IVP Books 2011

14. Beginning Contemplative Prayer, Out of Chaos into Quiet by Kathryn J. Hermes, Pauline Books and Media, Boston, 2009

15. Jesus Calling, Enjoying Peace in His Presence by Sarah Young, Thomas Nelson, 2004

16. The Breath of the Soul, Reflections on Prayer by Joan Chittister

17. The Way of Perfection by Saint Teresa of Avila, Translated and edited by E. Allison Peers

18. Mystical Paths to God: Three Journeys, The Practice of Presence of God, Interior Castle, Dark Night of the Soul by Brother Lawrence, Saint Teresa of Avila, and Saint John of the Cross

"Scripture taken from the NEW AMERICAN STANDARD BIBLE®, Copyright © 1960,1962,1963,1968,1971,1972,1973,1975,1977,1995 by The Lockman Foundation / Used by

Made in the USA
San Bernardino, CA
10 June 2016